MY POETIC THREADS
CREATE A TAPESTRY

CAROLYN JUNE-JACKSON

THE FOREWORD

"My Poetic Threads Create a Tapestry"

Websters Dictionary defines Tapestry as: "A fabric consisting of a warp upon which colored threads are woven by hand to produce a design, often pictorial, used for wall hangings, furniture coverings, etc. Tapestries are used to furnish, cover, or adorn."

I thought, how appropriate, this definition describing Carolyn June-Jackson's work and how a true wordsmith is always led to the right turn-of-phrase. The title is aptly descriptive and concise in its direct approach to expression. Her words paint upon the canvass of our minds and reveal vivid vistas of hope and expectation while reminding us of the deep valleys of despair into which we occasionally stumble.

Each stanza is akin to a thread woven through centuries of lives lived in color. Carolyn's poems are like the overcoats and blankets covering us during icy blizzards and white-out snowstorms. They comforted us when the wind came howling down the boulevard. Her poem, "*Papa Taught*," reminded me of how black men's hearts were sewn with courage, stitched with tenacity, and forged in determination's shop as they faced the perils of race hate and dehumanization under the guise of white supremacy. Her words in "*Me Too*" are weaved on a do-it-yourself loom, which speaks of intestinal fortitude as she slaps the face of any who would defile the sanctity of black women, which brought to remembrance why it can sometimes be challenging to make a black woman smile. She then reminds us of her royalty in "*A Black Queen Rules.*"

It has been my pleasure to wrap myself in the healing warmth created by the Tapestry of these poetic threads. It is written, "*In the beginning, was the Word and the Word was with God, and the Word was God.*"

After reading words in this Tapestry, which appear woven on a loom made in heaven, I am cloaked in a blanket of understanding, and I encourage all of you to turn the pages and warm yourself.

Ty Gray-EL

Storyteller, author, and recording artist

DEDICATION

I dedicate this book of poetry, "*My Poetic Threads Create a Tapestry*," to my husband Jerry aka JJ;

my parents, the late Charles and Florence (Beeks) June; siblings: brothers Claude aka Butch, Charles aka Michael, and James aka Stanley in his memory; sisters, Patricia aka Trisha, and Pauline, in her memory.

My maternal and paternal ancestors

Family matriarchs: Doris Little, the Beeks family matriarch, and mother-in-law Doretha Jackson, the Jackson family matriarch

Sisters-in-law, nephews, nieces, and god-children

Longest and dearest friend: Deborah Ruth in her memory; and

Spiritual mentors: Bishop Phillip and Lady Cindy Thomas

Last but certainly not least, I give honor to my Lord and Savior, Jesus Christ.

In 1981, it was the Spirit who prompted me to begin writing poetry. "*You have much to share, so share it.*"

ACKNOWLEDGMENTS

I am indebted to Ty Gray-El, for consenting to write the foreword to my book. Ty is a native of Washington, D.C. He is an internationally renowned storyteller, author, and recording artist who has dedicated his life to restoring the Africans' heritage and legacy in America. Ty is a two-time Spoken Word Billboard Award winner and critically acclaimed Poet Laureate of the African Diaspora. He is the Chief Spiritual Officer of Breath of My Ancestors, LLC. Follow him on Facebook under "*Breath of My Ancestors*" or visit his website at tygrayel.com to enjoy his eloquent and impactful poetic oratories. Because of poets like you, I am! Thank you, sir!

Lauren Dreux Carroll of LaLa Luvs Art of Oakland, California, designed my beautiful book cover. I shared my vision with Lauren, and she made it explicitly clear. Thank you so much for sharing your creative gift!

Joan Randall, Publisher, and CEO of Victorious You Press in Huntersville, North Carolina. Joan, a best-selling author, is a blessed sister in Christ, who coaches, prays, encourages, and patiently walks you through the publishing and marketing process. I was humbled when she told me my poetry book would be the first for her company, and she saw a second book following.

I look forward to our next collaboration.

I would be remiss if I didn't give a whoop-whoop to my family, friends, and, dare I say, followers. You have inspired and encouraged me since day one! Your words are like fuel to a fire, nectar to a bee, and rain during a drought. Every time you inspired me, you pushed me further along to where I am today...sharing my work with everyone!

Thank you for not allowing me to make excuses nor put down the pen!

INTRODUCTION

I chose for my title, "*My Poetic Threads Create a Tapestry*," because it accurately expresses how I envision my poetry: a hand-woven embroidered tapestry stitched together with strands of inspirational, realistic, humorous, and thought-provoking parables in rhyme.

As a teenager, I loved creating one-of-a-kind garments. When I matched the fabric with a complimentary spool of thread, I considered the type of cord and its weight. Performing this crucial step was necessary for a garment's tailored appearance and wearability. When I write, I use traditional appliqués to consider three things: (1) What I want to say? (2) How do I word it? and (3) Whose life will it touch?

When I share the obscene brutality and atrocities willfully carried out against the African Diaspora, I choose a woolly-type, coarse-textured thread because of its durability and superiority. Their God-given strength, courage, and endurance validated their survival during the Middle Passage and centuries of cruel and inhumane slavery.

When I reflect on my kinfolk's tapestry-laced life, I prefer polyester for its resiliency and longevity. My maternal and paternal grandparents set an example. They established a code of conduct that they passed on to their descendants on how to endure a systemic racist society; yet, overcome every obstacle placed before them to reap a full-filling life.

When I celebrate my sensuous and sassy sisters' black beauty and self-empowerment, I favor a silk-like, glossy thread that is smooth and not easily frayed, befitting our Nubian queens.

When I pay tribute to our priest, king, protector, and backbone, my clutch is a textured dual-duty thread because of its strength and smoothness for consistent tension. All honor to our black brothers!

When I boast on the hope of our at-risk young folks' potential and promise, I embrace nylon because of its resistance and stamina. They are our future, our hope, and our answer.

When I hand-weave poetry depicting historical, modern-day, political, or social mores of common folk and ordinary people, my fallback is a synthetic thread that is incapable of tangling and flawlessly blends my hand-stitched rhymes. I use a common thread of rich-tapestry-type expressions, powerful rhetoric, colloquial jargon, or writing in a vernacular they understand to lend warmth, texture, and color, ensuring my poetry is smooth, coherent, and concise.

I come from a lineage of writers, poets, actors, and public speakers. Our mama introduced us to Paul Laurence Dunbar's black dialect poetry while still in elementary school. As children, whenever we had writing or speaking assignments, she would remind us, "*When one word will do, don't make two.*"

Yes, mama, we always hear you!

As you read my poetic tapestry, I trust you find something educational, humorous, inspirational, or which you can relate to and embrace.

TABLE OF CONTENTS

SECTION ONE: AFRICA'S DIASPORA MOORISH TAPESTRY

SECTION TWO: KINFOLK'S BLENDED TAPESTRY

SECTION THREE: SISTERS' SILKY TAPESTRY

SECTION FOUR: BROTHERS' WOOLEN TAPESTRY

SECTION FIVE: YOUNG FOLKS' ECCENTRIC TAPESTRY

SECTION SIX: COMMON FOLK & ORDINARY PEOPLES' COPTIC TAPESTRY

SECTION ONE

AFRICA'S DIASPORA MOORISH TAPESTRY

Hated and mutilated because of our Nubian skin
Waited four centuries for captors to rectify their sins
Caught our ancestors sleeping, their spirit not unbroken
If you trespass, we warned you. Our Motherland has woken

America Ain't No Valentine

It's a new millennium; you think racism doesn't exist
I beg to differ with you; it remains a putrid cyst
Since the dawn of slavery, blatant racism was everywhere
We sat in the back of the bus but paid the same bus fare

In the 1960s, segregation was in most places
Forbidding anyone with kinky hair and sooty faces
They made us use the back door to get a chicken box
This slight was in the suburbs, not out in the boondocks

Pools, rinks, and theatres off-limits to ALL blacks
Stray into forbidden areas, got your hard head cracked
Never saw a "colored-only" sign; they were not that obvious
We stayed in our place, unlike Columbo, don't get curious

We didn't meet white kids until we went to middle school
Mingling was not encouraged, went against their rules
Long before the Movement, our rights kept out of range
In the 60s, schools integrated a few other laws made changes

Racists had convulsions when Obama became president
Celebrated in the streets when Trump made his ascent
He gave racists the green light to act any way they want
Harass and provoke us to show how ugly they could taunt

The evil eye of bigotry has been rubbed and poked
Make sure we don't forget that racism is no joke
We're still playing catch up; we don't have time to brag
Accept to let you know we will not wave a white flag

Our youth don't know the horrors of the angry white sharks
Yet, here we are again listening to deranged dogs' bark
They will be called the "n" word, don't let them grow up stupid
America ain't no Valentine; there's no such thing as cupid

Bury Us Deep

They say a chain is only as strong as its weakest link
Deny us an education doesn't mean we won't think
Like the slogan, "We Are Built Ford Tough" ®™
We grind differently when the going gets rough

Bury our contributions, denying us our greatness
We may desire peace but don't get in our business
Bury our female's ovaries, so we can't bear our seed
Saturate our embryos with coke, heroin, and weed

Bury our black men's dignity, drag them into court
Take away their income, so they can't pay child support
Bury our access to a fair trial; in a motion to dismiss
Planting false evidence. The truth will be our witness

Bury us up to our necks in a shallow sandy grave
We will dig ourselves out like those former slaves
Bury us in the topsoil as you would a hibiscus
We will come back to life like the old Jew Lazarus

Bury our vision of hope, so we'll be completely blind
Stifle our voices, but we still will speak our mind
Bury our civil rights like a "Birth of a Nation" sequel
Remember that six feet make every man an equal

Bury our sense of direction throw away the map
We will return your shovel polished and gift wrapped
Bury every generation, but a new one will arise
Burst through a clod of dirt with a fist toward the skies

Death Ship

They saw the slave ships converging from the pit of Hell
Familiar with their tall sails knew their origin too well
Came to kidnap a treasure, a human commodity
Transport Africans to a place called "the land of the free"

As the ships snaked closer, they saw their demonic mast
Anchors dropped in the abyss; the lot was cast
The drums reverberated for every tribe to hear
Warning every villager that danger had drawn near

Children torn from their father and mama's laps
The weak left behind would taste a leather strap
Those who refused the journey chose an eternity
Babies thrown against Weeping Boer Bean trees

The brave surrendered to begin the voyage overseas
The sickly would die due to their oppressor's rare disease
Slaves treated harshly like domestic animals or livestock
Like liquidated cash dragged to a foreign auction block

The trip turned into weeks. The distance was too far
Saltwater was used to rinse out their pulse-filled scars
The ever-present stench of death whippings often heard
The dead were thrown overboard without a prayerful word

The ship reached its port of call. Its profane flag raised
Those who made the voyage stood before a buyers' gaze
The ship remained in the harbor until the black ivory sold
Illegal contraband worth more than King Solomon's gold

Time had come for the ship to return by another route
No concern a Diaspora endured within the vessel's bowels
America, the beautiful, was built on black exploitation
Concealed their horror as they built their mighty nation

In memory of my ancestors who survived the Middle Passage

Go West!

God showed Abraham a land flowing with milk and honey
Satan gifted the Europeans America drenched with privilege
and money
God told his servant, Abraham, "*...as much as you see is yours*"
White settlers came to plunder both ends of the steaming shores

Immigrants arrived from overseas to claim an inheritance
Towns were burned down to the ground by racist militants
They acquired the Grand Canyon, comprised of its deep gorge
Staked a claim to the magnificent site as their coveted reward

Three-thousand miles stretched from one coast to the other
Enough land for every man to live peacefully with his brother
Sharing wasn't good enough; too much fertile land
Seized wastelands or swamps in case they could expand

Bounties on black landowners, some were former slaves
Rebuilt their towns and cities on top of unmarked graves
"*This land is our land from California to the New York Island*"
East or West of the Mississippi under their sovereign command

The Calvary drove the Indians out the changing of the guard
Used a form of genocide, banned from their tribal landmarks
The government parceled land with illegal homestead deals
Planted Old Glory in the soil where Indian's blood spilled

Drew red lines forbidding all men who did not favor them
Blacks forced into ghettos as the result of systemic racism
So, it has remained since the white man's mighty conquest
A manifest destiny campaign that enticed them to "Go West!"

I Still Can Criticize

Dragged to a country with cruel treatment undeserving
A white man's back and hands were worthy of preserving
Built this country on the black man's blood, sweat, and tears
Deny them inclusiveness in their preamble for many years

Author James Baldwin wrote, "*I have a right to criticize*"
A run-in with police means a minority most likely dies
They're often demeaned, disenfranchised, and demonized
Police shut off body cameras that will contradict their lies

Fast forward to the present, still too much racial tension
Under no circumstances make minorities their equivalent
Blacks marched for civil rights made minimal progress
Sixty years passed, still feeling somewhat oppressed

A revolution in America released a giant gorilla
Racists who bear arms are known as militia killers
The odor of hate is pungent as a crate of rotten eggs
Whine when blacks can't walk after breaking their legs

We protest police brutality; society says we're wrong
In response to defunding, they are more headstrong
Escalating agitation shield domestic terrorist antics
Refuse to aide protesters assaulted by racist fanatics

Black lives do matter the cry from whites and blacks
Police look the other way when the Proud Boys attack
A malfeasant is in the White House spews hateful lies
Although Trump was not my choice, I still can criticize

Juneteenth, Our Day of Emancipation

In 1619, cargo arrived in a small city called Jamestown
The trouble with this cargo it was chained and bound
An illegal civil war left southerners dead in its wake
The North beat the South, who had too much at stake

America chose July 4, 1776, to celebrate its independence
The enslaved treated with compassionless indifference
Blacks waited for release from their incarceration
June 19, 1865, was chosen as their real emancipation

The Emancipation Proclamation signed by Abraham Lincoln
Freeing the slaves caused a bittered contention
Slave owners saw free labor slipping from their grasp
States south of the Mason-Dixon Line saw economic collapse

Slaves understood the South's loss and financial disaster
They were too afraid to leave the property of their masters
The decree did not reach Texas; blacks still locked away
Three years before Galveston released their human prey

Former slaves observed this milestone in their history
Some called it Jubilee Day, a long-awaited victory
Juneteenth is symbolic of self-rule and liberty
Delayed but not denied from Dixie's tyranny

Return to the Mall

In 1963, the whole nation gathered
Declaring our civil rights did matter
Arm in arm, they marched together
Despite the humid August weather

Took buses and domestic flights
Marched to the beat of civil rights
Converged on the National Mall
It was all for one and one for all

Folks from poverty to upper class
No barking dog, batons, or tear gas
Marched for a more significant cause
Repealing every evil Jim Crow law

The leader, Martin Luther King
Declared to all, "Let freedom ring"
His famous speech, "I Had a Dream"
Will our liberties be redeemed?

Fifty years have come and gone
Again, they gathered on the lawn
A distractor showing no restraint
Profaned the site with loud green paint

The planned purpose remains the same
Right history's wrongs will be our aim
We have come again, lifting our voice
March and protest for equal choice

That Would Be a No!

You say ugly words you hope will make us cringe
Terrorizing and taunting will keep us unhinged
We are too wise and savvy to pay much attention
To your racist tone, so I guess we should mention

Our ancestors were royalty; so, don't you get it twisted
Given two-thirds of the world; in caves, your race existed
Dragged us here in chains against our will or consent
Now, demand that we return to a distant continent

Descendants came to Virginia long before Ellis Island
You used them as free labor, offering them no asylum
We don't care what you say or what you believe
We will squat on this land until we choose to leave

Wrap yourself in your rebel flag sing six bars of Dixie
But don't get in our faces unless you are feeling risky
We will raise our fists and scream "*no, not ever again*"
Don't step to us with threats; our skin is not that thin

The tar babies have gotten too big for your cradle
Assuming we were scared was always your fable
We are not trespassers with no right to be here
After we picked your cotton, then you stole the frontier

From our Indian brothers who first settled this land
You're the real interloper with your bogus demands
Sent in the calvary to evict them in broad daylight
Threw your weight about like it was your birthright

Now you clown at hate rallies belligerent and bold
Will never persuade us to move from our zip code
Spitting and screaming like a demon-possessed
It won't entice us to fill out a forwarding address

No slaughtering us like poor young Emmet Teal
Those who mutilated him did so for a thrill
Burn a cross in my yard; you'll get jailed for arson
Spray painting property is now old fashion

In the middle of a room stands a racist elephant
Make America Great Again is so irrelevant
Those bygone days have ended. Take a look around
BLM is on the plaza; General Robert E. Lee is down

You're nobody's landlord. You best think again
Property taxes paid up, so you get in the wind
What we plan to do is line up at a voting booth
Get rid of Trump's lies replace them with truth

Most of us won't waste time holding our breath
Mitch McConnell doesn't care about our health
Trump is running this country like a mafia Cartel
He can move to Mar-a-Lago and rule his private hell

We Are Africa

Observe our features, see the tribal scars on our face
You can't deny our genesis, ethnicity, or race
Touch our hair, our nose, and kiss our lips
Can't you see God's image in his workmanship?

Can ancestry dot com trace our branches and deep roots?
Would it be our reality that no one could dispute?
Matching every leaf of our diverse family tree
Undergo an excavation to unearth our mystery

Ancient history is unrivaled; handed down by the scribes
An untainted pure-blooded race of every African tribe
While our ancestors studied science, math, and fine arts
Europeans left their caves to tear our motherland apart

God created this vast earth dividing the real estate
To his dark-skinned creation gave his best to dominate
Expansive is our continent consumes most of the earth
A far-reaching span of land bequeathed to them since birth

God rocked his raisin babies in the cradle of civilization
In their bloodline rest the lifeblood of every great nation
The shades of our skin tone extend the color spectrum
Under microscopes, scientists studied our rare melanin

Vanilla to dark chocolate, diverse as Ben and Jerry's
Our DNA is as complex as Dr. Albert Einstein's theory
Families separated once they reached the promised land
Sold together or as singles, illegal human contraband

We are hated and mutilated because of our Nubian skin
Waiting now four centuries for captors to rectify their sins
Caught our ancestors sleeping, their spirit not unbroken
If you trespass, we warned you. Our Motherland has woken

We Are Not the People

The phrase, "*We, the People*," was not meant for us
Viewed as evil and brutal, treated with disgust
Abused by the slave master victims of their racist lies
Undesired foreigners deprived and disenfranchised

The founding fathers vowed to "*advocate for justice*"
Ignored those from the wombs of their black mistresses
"*Imperfect beings*" denied a part of "*their perfect union*"
Descendants of the framers would inherit all dominion

To promote "*peace of mind factored in tranquility*"
No regard for a bondservant viewed as property
Signers added a provision for "*a common defense*"
The slave wants inclusion; the owners took offense

Upgrade "*general welfare*" to benefit white supremacy
A slave's descendant relies on social welfare to infinity
Our framers wrote "*secure the blessings of liberty and posterity*"
Architects of the preamble left the slave out of "*We*"

SECTION TWO

KINFOLK'S BLENDED TAPESTRY

Early in the morning, her singing hit the rafters
Quickly got annoyed if we burst into laughter
Mama prayed each night, despite the day's events
Her head bowed low; the room dispersed a holy scent

Crossing the Finish Line

As soon as the official discharged his gun
Val and other participants began their run
It may be a 20K marathon in a frosty chill
One-third of those twenty miles all uphill

Val sets off slowly to save her precious wind
Start too quickly may make her head spin
She sets a consistent pace easy to maintain
As a senior, she knows she's no G.I. Jane

Val maintains her physical shape for marathons
She ran five miles a day up at the crack of dawn
No matter what the weather forecast revealed
She does stretch and squats even hits the treadmill

Val ran a half or whole marathon in each state
No small feat forty-nine marathons to date
Mark, her husband, and biggest fan, often joins in
They both run the distance though neither might win

In January 2020, Hawaii will be Val's tour de force
She is now in training plans to finish the course
Marathons are demanding, but she couldn't resist
Checking off this milestone from her bucket list

Dedicated to my cousin, Valerie Hunter-Kelly, who realized her dream of finishing a half or full marathon in all fifty states! She completed her final marathon in Hawaii in January 2020! Regrettably, we lost Val to cancer on November 7, 2020.

Don't Fence Me In!

At three, I climbed a chain-link fence
Must have lacked good common sense
I can't recall making a choice
To ignore my mama's voice

Too young to detect right from wrong
I resolved to finish strong
My little heart was not afraid
In a dress, hair up in braids

Though the fence was very tall
I took my time and scaled the wall
Must make it to the other side
If I fail, at least I tried

I lost one shoe but didn't stop
Finally made it to the top
To my mama's poor chagrin
I would do it all again

The way I always climb a fence
I did it at my own expense
Despite all of our earthly time
We all will have a fence to climb

*A childhood accomplishment

Doris' Birthday Bash

We had a great big party for Aunt Doris Saturday night
Since it was her 80th, we set it off just right
Shut your mouth! Weren't you invited? It must have been an
oversight!
Then I won't say much about it; that would be too impolite

Her daughters plan a party and did not spare expense
Neighbors living next door even jumped a chain-link fence
You needed no grand title like a madam or sir
If your name was on the list, then you showed up as you were

Doris' sister Irene made an entrance fit for a queen
The party can commence since she is on the scene
Family and friends assembled to wish Doris the best
Some she barely knew dropped by out of respect

Folks from off the beltway start showing up at noon
The out-of-town guests would turn the corner soon
Her colleagues from Eastern Market showed up in a van
They were late arriving had to close their vending stand

Tami yells, "*Come and get it*," we gathered around to eat
Doris took her place in the guest of honor seat
Soul food served on china and in lovely crystal bowls
Silver-plated flatware sets wrapped in linen rolls

The table spread so lavishly made you glad it was a treat
Debra asked, "*Who cleaned the chitlins?*" as she gazed at the
feast
Carved roast beef and fried chicken made you lick your lips
Collards with smoked neck bones--bless my soul—was worth a
trip

There indeed were aplenty, double portions all around
Lots of Perry's sweet ice tea to wash each morsel down
The only thing to bring was an unfed appetite
We commence to chowing down on everything in sight

Shelia presents a birthday cake that's longer than a sidearm
So many candles burning, it set off two smoke alarms
Doris shuts her eyes and leans back to make a wish
Heaven sake! A store-bought cake? Where's mama's cobbler
dish?

Next came the tributes as we each took turns to speak
Some were so long-winded, swore for grits; it took all week
So that the guest of honor could say what's on her mind
Meant we had to cut it off or we would run out of time

Doris starts sharing about those days in Honea Path
When she and all her siblings had to take a Saturday bath
Toting buckets from the well, pulling water up the shaft
Church on Sunday morning or they felt their papa's wrath

Hot mornings picking cotton in the Carolina heat
Evenings sitting on the porch soaking blistered feet
Hitch old Sally to a wagon and down the road, they went
Then arrive in time for supper and an afternoon well spent

If you did not do your chores, you would do them after dark
The school was not a hangout; best bring home good marks
As she continues thinking about those by-gone days
Daughter Angie puts in a CD, and music starts to play

Angie led the soul train line, hips swaying roundabout
We fall right in behind her, blowing whistles in our mouths
Tried to get the birthday girl to join the dancing line
Aunt Doris went to bed; it was half-past nine

*A tribute to Doris Beeks-Little, the Beeks family matriarch

Granny's Quilted Stories

Granny gathered what I called old faded-out rags
Every piece of scrap kept in plastic recycled bags
"*Don't throw it away*," she'd say. "*It's part of history*"
Every swatch she hoarded had an extraordinary story

She learned how to patchwork when she was barely eight
Her mama told her daughter do not forget its weight
If the quilt is bulky, it will be too hard to clean
Sew it too thin or sparse; it will unravel at the seams

Granny used a cotton thread, made sure that it would hold
She might opt for subtle colors unless her choice was bold
Collected velvet, cotton, linen, old lace from a wedding dress
Handwash every swatch; make sure each piece is pressed

"*Those youngins will cheat stitch on fancy sewing machines
I only need thread and a needle to keep my edges clean*"
Sucked her teeth at a tape measure – eyeballed a perfect line
Careful to trim the edges, so they all matched up just fine

Granny once stitched a quilt that told a horrendous story
Klansmen shot her papa sent his spirit straight to Glory
Left him out on a dusty road with six children and a spouse
After dark, his sons carried his corpse back to the house

They never knew who shot her papa, much less went to jail
Salty tears fell on her patchwork as she told her sorrowful tale
The ragged hand-made relics now ruined by moths and mildew
Each quilt had its story that granny once lived through

In memory of Nancy James-Beeks, my maternal grandmother

Papa Taught

Papa had those steel-gray eyes
Barely schooled but very wise
Proud to be a country boy
Children were his pride and joy

He was tall, lean, and fit to fight
Could put his enemies to flight
Lived his life on right and wrong
Taught offspring to get along

Taught both sons to use a gun
Put troublemakers on the run
When the Klan came on his land
He kept his shotgun close at hand

Taught them how to plow a field
Harvest crops to make hot meals
Taught that life is more worth livin'
If love and trust are always given

Taught them always to keep their word
Don't spread ugly things they heard
Showed them that it's wrong to steal
Give every man an honest deal

Taught them that good credit counts
If they owe someone, keep low amounts
Taught them to love the Lord
Doing right earns its reward

Papa was a self-made man
On his beliefs, he took a stand
A man's man one of a kind
Walked ahead, never behind

In memory of Claude Beeks, maternal grandfather (1883-1966)

She Lived Her Eulogy

If you write Florence Etta's story, don't forget to tell it right
Grandma Nancy's shadow didn't let her out of sight
Always on her heels mocked her walk and stance
She never cared for worldly music nor even learned to dance

Read her first poetry book. Mama's world opened wide
Cherished each word and phrase hidden deep inside
Memorizing verses of her favorite poetic author
She never dreamt in black and white, but in living color

Avoided escalators and airplanes, never learned to drive
Could stand before an audience with a voice that amplifies
She slipped into her zone when it was time to read her part
Eloquent, articulate, the words poured from her heart

Forever in the background, no guile did she have
Not one to be pretentious; with her soft as cotton laugh
At sixty-five, a milestone, we gave a birthday party
Treated her like a queen for she was our royalty

She never met a stranger; kind words stayed in her mouth
If you thought she was a friend, you never had to doubt
Precious as the day was long sweet as she could be
Rebuked a liar or talebearer, she believed in honesty

Early in the morning, her singing hit the rafters
Quickly got annoyed if we burst into laughter
Mama prayed each night, despite the day's events
Her head bowed low. The room released a holy scent

She studied the word of God, able to defend the bible
Not one to waste time, sleep too late, nor be found idle
A walking eulogy, she also talked the talk
Her mantra was to live upright, cling to her Living Rock

In memory of Florence Etta Beeks-June, my mother (1916-2002)

We (Our Wedding Vows)

Before God and man, we stood unified
Family and friends let no one set aside
God as our Keeper, love as our guide
Naysayer chants dissipate like a tide

I take you to be my partner for life
To live our purpose as husband and wife
We promise to share our earthly wealth
For richer or poorer, in sickness and health

We pledge our faith in God's Holy will
Every promise we make, we commit to fulfill
Each vow we make, we will put to a test
Forsake all others without any regret

We commit to support, respect, and obey
Affirm to each other our love every day
As we walk together, our dreams will unfold
For better or worse, to have and to hold

Rings exchanged will serve as a token
Cherished memento with words unspoken
A tradition befitting a moment like this
To seal these nuptials with a kiss

We'll look back on this day after years gone by
Search for love in each other's eyes
I give to you freely the gift of my heart
To love you forever until death do us part

*Dedicated to my husband, Jerry, on our wedding day –
November 8, 2015*

SECTION THREE

SISTERS' SILKY TAPESTRY

"I will keep this simple, give you a piece of advice
Don't run up on a sister. Some aren't very nice
If you bum-rush a black queen, who is without her crown
You will find yourself recouping from a relentless beat down"

50th High School Class Reunion

I got an invite, followed up by a phone call
To our 50th class reunion, come one and all
The event takes place on the 20th of July
If you plan to grace the place, return a reply

I called on my besties with whom I kept in touch
If they plan to go, make it a girls' trip, and such
The class committee organized all the tours
Take in the nightlife and incredible sights for sure

Dust off my yearbook, match name with a face
Good and bad memories only time could erase
I wonder what they look like if they changed a lot
Still got those slim bodies or a face that time forgot

I decided I would purchase a slinky black dress
Match the shoes and accessories, not look a hot mess
When I finished high school, I sprinted like a marathon
Been clocking in at Bell Atlantic, now renamed Verizon®

We turned up super early. Most had not arrived
When our crew rolls in, we shift to overdrive
All my classmates changed; they wore their class photo
The popular guys we remembered were strolling in solo

The homecoming queen's Botox lips rivaled a bass®
The homecoming king approached a few for cash
Grooved to Motown music, all the steps we learned
Smooth Fred Astaire moves followed with fancy turns

They stocked the bar; the drinking line was long
Then the class president begins to slur the old school song
No one remembers the words, but we tried anyhow
Disrupted by a brawl when a guest called his wife a cow

Some weird guy from our class ran by us in the buff
The event starts to wind down. I have had enough
We got our wraps, said goodbye, headed for the door
No more class reunions returned the dress I wore

*Dedicated to the Class of '68 alumni

A Beautiful Scar

The mirror caught the scar, which hadn't been an issue
It was keloid and linear with overlaid scar tissue
I mused over its origin, memories of the injury
A long-ago reminder of pain and misery

As I sat for a moment, my mind drifted back
To the date, time, and place of the vicious attack
Hanging out with friends as young girls often do
We broke a rule we knew was already a taboo

Someone said, "*let's play a game of hide-n-seek*"
Our game was not for the timid or the meek
We'd sneak to our hiding place with a few playmates
I can't miss my curfew, which was half-past eight

If you engage in the game, you needed steady nerves
Tangled in the thickets, you got what you deserved
Like fairies, we ran straight into the backwoods
The area was so haunting, and hiding was so good

The moon shined bright, giving off a radiant light
You could not be afraid to play this game at night
I spied a friend peeking from behind a rotted tree
She was in my crosshairs, wouldn't get the best of me

I crept behind a brush tried to catch her by surprise
Stumbled over a fallen limb was soon immobilized
Felt over my body, making sure each part was intact
I sensed I'd done some damage executing an acrobat

Down the front of my face, blood flowed like a river
Instinctively knew there would be a scar forever
I ran straight to mama with blood covering my eyes
On the way home, I rehearsed my little lie

I made up a tale that was far-fetched and extreme
I didn't fool mama with my rather devious scheme
When she saw I required immediate medical attention
She took me to the emergency to ward off an infection

I've had this beautiful scar for as long as I can remember
It has been a reminder that I tripped over some timber
When I became a woman, a love tore my heart apart
The result of a cheater who left a deep scar on my heart

*Dedicated to my playmates who are now deceased

Aretha, A Rose is Still a Rose

Born in Memphis, Tennessee, a child prodigy
A caramel-skinned girl who was a classic beauty
One could never overlook her God-given voice
At the age of sixteen, easily the people's choice

Aretha sang genres like gospel, classical, and R&B
Accompanied by blues, pop, soul, or a symphony
Her sultry lyrics moaned, "*You did me wrong*"
If she coughed, it became a top billboard song

Earned her title as Queen of Soul in 1968
Many of her diva counterparts would abdicate
The first female chose to Rhythm/Blues Hall of Fame
Even her haters had to admit Aretha was the game

R-E-S-P-E-C-T record was her first number one hit
What you want, she had it; what you need, she got it
In her pink Cadillac, she was in the driver's seat
Awarded eighteen Grammys was no small feat

If Re-Re requested your presence, you would attend
Everyone wanted to become her personal friend
She hid her privacy, not one to run her mouth
Over a sixty-year reign, she did not once hit a drought

In Detroit's Motor City, she was its golden girl
That commanding voice took her around the world
Entertained presidents, the pope, and Buckingham
She was flattered whenever introduced as a madam

What you spent to hear her bring down the timber
A performance of that caliber you would remember
God entombed that voice. It is under lock and key
Can it be replicated; it's up to God, but why would He?

Black Queen Rules

A black queen sits on her majestic throne
There is no doubt she can hold her own
She would always place in a beauty contest
Stands head and shoulders above the rest

Her bloodline is cobalt blue, with no impurities
Each pore exudes nobility, no insecurities
She won't mince words with a joker or a clown
Secure enough to adjust another queen's crown

Diadem overlaid with gems, not too heavy to carry
She extends a scepter if he is her choice to marry
He inhales a scent of Jasmine from her devouring fire
Two dynasties consummate to build a mighty empire

An admirer wins her heart boast he has a costly find
While others calibrate their game or get left behind
Boldly shields her dominion and stands her ground
He is unworthy if he can't keep what he has found

She interned her suiter like a quarry within her snare
No question he's the one who could protect her lair
Seduced by her ebony beauty and her siren's voice
In the depths of his soul, he felt he had no choice

BLM to Sassy

My name is Sassy, aka Sassafras!

Well, they done killed George Floyd!

Yep, a racist officer pressed his white knee onto George's black neck until he stopped breathing. In broad daylight! He forced George to eat tar and gravel for 8 minutes, 46 seconds (in handcuffs). Then the rabid racist had the gall to look directly into a video cell phone as if to say, "*I'm going to Disneyworld!*"

Over $20! I would have given the clerk a bill if I had been there. "*Brother, I got you.*" No need to summon the Boogaloo Boys.

Now, I haven't spent much time in Sunday school since I was a kid, but when George cried out to his mama, it was like when, in his humanity, Jesus cried out to the Father, "*Why has thou forsaken me?*"

And when George said his final words, "*I can't breathe,*" It was as if Jesus, from His Divinity, said, "*It is finished.*" *I was going in y'all!*

My name is Sassy, aka Sassafras.

I'm tired; we are tired. Four hundred years of being tired! And when the rest of the world witnessed the diabolical act, they were angry, sick, and tired.

And we are traumatized by the abuse and killings of black people at the hands of racist sociopaths posing as public defenders. More like offenders if you ask anybody my color!

It's hard to watch the news, listen to the radio, surf the Internet, or read a newspaper.

I'll admit I have been encouraged by the protests; marches in fifty states, the District of Columbia, and all around the world shouting police brutality among minorities must stop!

Black Lives Do Matter!

The size of the crowds was mind-blowing! It was like guessing the number of jelly beans in a jar...Black, White, Hispanics, Asians, American Indians from every tribe and tongue. It was an incredible sight! I even saw the Amish standing on the sidelines with their signs! It looked like they stepped out of the 19th century. You know they have limited contact with the outside world, so I'm wondering who told them? It was as if they said, "*We got you, my brothers and sisters!*"

We tried to be peaceful, but those hateful right-wing provocateurs instigated by spray painting buildings, looting, and setting fires under the BLM cause.

But what they weren't going to do was spray paint Missy Sally's Bar-b-que Ribs and Brisket Barn down on the Pike with Sherman Williams paint samples or torch it...we won't have it! Missy Sally has been up in that piece since I was in grade school! Plus, my Uncle Stanley works there. He calls himself a sous-chef, but he just makes steak and cheese subs.

Sorry, where was I?

On Saturday, I got up early to participate in the protest on the plaza. They said to be there no later than 8:00 am. I wanted to get in the mix, so I took the subway and a #10 bus because there was no need to drive. There was no place to park.

We marched for twenty blocks, across the 14th Street bridge, through the Southwest Freeway tunnel, over the Potomac River, and through the woods around the Tidal Basin. People from every coalition twenty feet wide and stretched for miles. "*I saw a number no man could number.*" There I go quoting scripture again.

By 2:00 p.m., we were marching, chanting, and singing like we got a five-day eviction notice, no employment, and our stimulus check got lost in the mail. We chanted, "*Remember George,*" "*I Can't Breathe,*" and "*No Justice, No Peace.*" And some more stuff, I can't repeat.

The National Guard was there, too. President Trump's gopher, Attorney General Bill Barr, sent them down to Lafayette Square to babysit us and make sure we didn't bum rush the White House. At the same time, "The Orange One" hid down in his bunker! He ordered fencing around the perimeter, too. The only thing missing was a moat!

We caught a high pulling down those old confederate statues - symbols of hate and slavery. And, if the person was on a horse, we pulled down Trigger too! And when we couldn't pull them down, we marked them up with some permanent paint we brought along! They pulled Christopher Columbus off his stand and tossed him in the Potomac River. Christopher now sleeps with the fishes. It was gangsta!

The Sons and Daughters of the Confederacy lost their minds! I say, let them put those statues in their front yard as an ornament like the folks with those commemorative pandas back in 2012. Unfortunately, some of the figures ended up in a hundred little pieces.

Police officers are walking off the job, protesting, or taking early retirement. They say that if they can't choke or beat the crap out of black men or women, they might as well quit. They don't want their cases re-opened. Of course, I'm paraphrasing. But I say, good riddance. Do security at the Dollar General.

I was good for the first five miles. When my feet began burning, the sun situated straight up in the sky, the temperature hit 90 degrees. I sat my frail self down before I slid down because heat and I barely speak as it is.

Police pepper-sprayed and shot at us with rubber bullets. I hurried up and got my backside out of there.

I arrived home, looking for a little sympathy; I told my mama what happened. She said I had no business downtown getting caught up in all that foolishness. I should have known better. Mama is scared of everything. She wouldn't even join a picket line of parents when the School Board threatened to stop serving pizza. She refused to attend the March on Washington in 1963!

Organizers texted us to return the next day for another twenty-mile hike and eight hours of speeches. No, I don't think so! Ms. Sassy will be at home, soaking her bunions and watching CNN. And I got to wash my masks!

We want reparation and fair and equal treatment on EVERY level. And, we want something done about the rotten fruit on the police force and police unions. I don't like guns, but I'll buy myself a Glock with a pearl handle from Benny's Pawn Shop on Culpeper and Lee Highway to protect me and mine! Trust me!

George, your death sparked a raging fire that can't be distinguished. Because, like your baby girl said, "*Daddy changed the world.*"

If WE don't get NO justice, trust, and believe, THEY won't get NO peace!!

I already told you my name is Sassy, aka Sassafras. I'm done!

Brown Caramel and Black Licorice

Our skin color is not the only reason we're so pretty
Candy-coated chocolate infused with rich toffee
We are dark and potent like black licorice
Men crave our luscious taste and bite off a piece

Our center is creamy smooth no one can dispute
Break open the middle; you will find luscious fruit
We are Almond Joy, Chocolate Kiss, and Baby Ruth®
The most delectable, juiciest, and mouthwatering truth

A sampler's sweet tooth, a delicious treat
Milk, white, dark, ruby, Belgian, or bittersweet
It may keep you up at night bouncing off a wall
When it runs its course, you will be in free fall

Despite the flavor, there are a few side effects
Candy destroys your teeth like nicotine cigarettes
Loss of sleep, nervousness, and head migraines
The sugary delight can also cause a weight gain

So, be careful if you want to sample our delicacy
If you are unable to abstain from celibacy
We are hard to ignore if your mouth wants to taste
Oh, the damage it does when the zits hit your face

Chocolate Diamond

Our porcelain skin is distinctively dark
Though some see it as an ugly birthmark
Melanin is opulent of unmatched worth
Queen Sheba's daughters, of royal birth

Tight, natural hair is a gift from the Nile
Not that artificial Brazilian hairstyle
Lips ripe and plump, an enticing enchantment
We don't require Botox or any enhancements®

We are an original, not anyone's carbon copies
Because a holy God created our unique bodies
Hips are voluptuous. Thighs not modified
To carry a toddler on one hip, they are extra wide

Your mocking says that black girls are deformed
Our Nubian looks are far from the white norm
We are unique and complete in God's holy image
You tell the Potter that his work is blemished

Crown and Glory

Most don't know the origin of our crown and glory
So, I will take a moment to translate its story
This ancestral headpiece is thousands of years old
They are uniquely worn, a queenly sight to behold

From 1640-1865, they were a fabric of enslavement
An effort on the owner's part to make a rude statement
Our men are known to wear a kufi in various colors
But tignons are worn by the women, not the brothers

Racists desire to disrespect or denounce our culture
To dishonor our rich past, present, and future
They are intimidated by a well-wrapped crown
But they need to woosah and calm down

We wear our crowns in honor of our history
Not wrapped like mammy, as a form of mockery
Slaves weren't seen as equal and always oppressed
No racism could stop us from wearing a headdress

A symbol of refined nobility, religion, or success
Wraps represent modesty, our origin, our progress
A celebration of African womanhood tied in a twist
It is a strong cultural statement, so don't criticize it

The headwrap is worn to complement an attire
Uniquely wrapped turbans are what we desire
Wraps are for special events or fashion displays
It comes in handy as a covering on a bad hair day

Women who love headwraps get viciously attacked
If worn out in public, the wearer may catch some flack
Bigots see the head covering as political defiance
A sister may get terminated if not in compliance

It is revolutionary, respected, and indeed renowned
We are proud of our headwraps. A queenly coiffed crown
It depicts our royal bloodline; we don't need to explain
Styles may come and go, but our headpiece remains

Dear Young Black Sistahs

Your beauty is unmatched in all the earth
Others salivate at your lovely features from birth
Society applies pressure to look like other human beings
Attempt to make you ashamed of your ancestral genes

Always have an opinion be as intelligent as can be
It's not your concern that at the root is insecurity
Don't be willing to dumb down; let your intelligence shine
Only a person with your I.Q. cares what's behind your hairline

Suppressed feelings or emotions is not what this is about
Let others know you have a voice without acting out
If they can't handle how you excel in your academics
It's not your fault they struggle and unfamiliar with phonics

We tend to choose men because we think they are cute
Low self-esteem or immaturity is most likely the root
Don't fall for stuffed toy animals and restaurant dinners
Find a grown man who's secure and acts like he's a winner

You are a survivor, and most battles you will conquer
What does not kill you will surely make you stronger
See a glass half full or sip from an overflowing cup
When your world is upside down, it's right side up

Dedicated to my lovely nieces

Do You!

If you want to describe me, what would you say
Stand on a soapbox and shout accolades all-day
Brag on my qualities, gifts, talents, and attributes
Then stick a knife in my back; even the blind can't refute

First, you compliment me, heap on lots of praise
Then use toxic words like a stick match to set me ablaze
Because you are intimidated and too insecure
To make yourself look good, smear my name like manure

You thought an alliance with me would earn you acclaim
You lack my charisma, and you don't have my game
No need to compete. We are not on an equal plane
Don't try to link your caboose to my train

It's a bone of contention when you fight for attention
You will get hypertension trying to be my competition
Be satisfied with who God created you to be
Imitation is not flattery if you're imitating me

Fight for Love

So, in love, she only saw what she wanted to see
Though she did see a glimpse of his insanity
She misread subtle signs ignored the red flags
He wished to see her laid out in a body bag

He needed to control her with a burst of anger
Not once did she see him as imminent danger
He would often beat her like a piece of wood
She defended him said he was misunderstood

Friends confided that not only was he a flirt
He beat his last girlfriend for burning his shirt
Just because she wanted out of the relationship
The real reason she slipped from his tight grip

Mind games hadn't worked, so fighting commenced
The men in her family were visibly incensed
They warned, "*Get out before he does more harm*"
Due to ruptured eardrums, she couldn't hear the alarm

Kept physical abuse silent and under close wraps
She decided to speak up when he finally snaps
Used every excuse in the book why she couldn't retreat
Until he sliced her brown face down to the pink meat

Safety became more costly than anything she owned
She planned to leave him, the three cats, and her home
Now thanks to her family, friends, and God above
That convinced her she never has to fight for love

If you are a victim of domestic violence
Do not ignore red flags or be forced into silence
If there's any form of abuse you choose to ignore
What you tolerate now will escalate to much more

*Dedicated to all the victims of physical, emotional, and mental domestic violence

Gratuity

I left the job after working late one night
Before turning in, I stopped for a bite
It's never my choice to eat out alone
I prefer ordering door dash on my cellphone

Visit my little cafe, a neighborhood place
I slid into a booth with my leather briefcase
I chose an appetizer, lobster spring rolls
While others watched the super bowl

While perusing a menu to order an entrée
In walked a herd of sisters dressed to slay
Spent hours at both nail and beauty salon
Talking real ghetto and smacking on gum

Acting ratchet like they were from the hood
They consumed lots of drinks not too much food
Loud and wired released a flood of estrogen
Their bar bill finally equaled two Benjamins

At closing time, they asked for their tab
Luckily, they held back enough for a cab
You would've thought the bill was an obituary
When one hollers out, " *Who ordered a gratuity?*"

Harriet Tubman

Harriet Tubman was a wanted female slave runner
In the dead of night, she outwitted bounty hunters
She ran an Underground Railroad like it was a train
If slaves trusted Harriet, they'd never see slavery again

She was born a slave on Maryland's Eastern Shore
Led three hundred to freedom was not folklore
Tired of the harsh treatment she received as a slave
It gave her courage, taught her to be bold and brave

She sustained a head injury when she was in her teens
Suffered from headaches, seizures, and dreams
It worked in her favor. She said she spoke to God
She boasted to the other slaves He was Moses' rod

Nineteen return trips led her family and strangers out
There was always the threat of danger lurking about
When slaves became weary or overcome with fear
She threatened, "*Walk, or I will shoot you right here!*"

Harriet earned the nickname "Moses" after a Jewish man
Stay ahead of bounty hunters was her best-laid plan
There was no turning back; she knew for sure
A dosage of freedom was the only miracle cure

Some kind-hearted people treated her like family
Abolitionist John Brown or reformer Susan Anthony
She was a cook for the Union Army, a nurse, and a spy
Each time she headed North, she told the South goodbye

In 1913, when she passed surrounded by friends and family
Thankful she died a hero and not hung from a tree
Interred as "General Tubman" at Fort Hill Cemetery
Among noted leaders, she was a true revolutionary

Her Iconic Voice

She strolled on center stage as if gliding on ice
A recipient of Grammy awards more than twice
You could hear a pin drop; the audience was so attentive
Just breathing the same air was an honored incentive

Maya Angelou, poet laureate, a lady of grace
A bold voice hit a crescendo when it permeated a place
Her curvaceous lips part, exposing a captivating smile
She could hypnotize, mesmerize, transfix you for a while

She asked a rhetorical question; you would want to reply
If her voice were a drug, you would have cannabis high
We grasped each intimacy and expressive nuance she unveiled
Savoring the fragrance of a honeysuckle voice as it exhaled

She eloquently paints words on canvas like a work of art
While unashamedly and blatantly revealing a painful heart
Her words so inspiring, captivating and profound
The deaf could read her lips had she not made a sound

Transparent and crystal clear, not one to hide her fears
A voice so soothing it would move a narcissist to tears
Before "*I Know Why the Caged Bird Sings*" and "*Still I Rise*"
Some never knew Maya was assaulted and left traumatized

Angelou was larger than life and in a class all by herself
Never blamed her hardships on the world or no one else
A voice resonating as loud as a percussionist's gong
Fervently and cogently condemning society's wrongs

In "*Phenomenal Women*," she shares where her beauty lies
Making inferences: "*flash of my teeth*" or "*fire in my eyes*"
A diversity of awards; praise, and accolades shown
What we admire most was that iconic voice was known

*A tribute to one of my favorite female poets, Maya Angelou,
Poet Laureate*

Just Call Me Sassy

Mama named me Sassy, aka Sassafras, after the tea!

When I asked about my name, she said my long body pushing on her diaphragm gave her indigestion during pregnancy. Sassafras tea was the only thing that settled the acid reflux!

I got above average looks like your sister or first cousin!

I do have a beautiful shape! And I know how to flirt in my halter and booty skirt!

Mama said, "*Sassy, you're beautiful in your way, but your beauty comes from what's in your heart and your head. Beauty won't make you any money.*" She's right. I stay broke as a joke. Sometimes I'm not happy with who I am. I wish I could have been someone else.

I should have been Katherine Johnson.

I love math and science and excelled in algebra, geometry, and physics. And I could send men into orbit!

I earned good grades, which kept me out of trouble. I received a full scholarship to an HBCU. But my mind got entangled with boys like a five-n-dime kite in a schizophrenic breeze.

Yea, I WAS good at math and science, but I now work as a night manager at a Dairy Delight down on Route 50!

Mama said, "*Sassy, you talk too much. You are still running your mouth. Keep wagging your tongue. Whose business are you minding now? You never could hold water!*"

I got it honest. I was listening to mama stand around on the church grounds after service "gossiping" while we were starving and ready to go home!

Maybe I could have been a White House news correspondent like April Ryan or Yamiche Alcindor.

They are quick with the tongue and dishing dirt. When April and Yamiche collide with Trump, he is crawling from a four-car pile-up! As quiet as it's kept, he's scared of strong, black intelligent women!

Yes, I got a sassy mouth, too. But I'm careful about what I say because mama may now be in heaven, but she can still reach down and slap me silly!

Anyway, I would have been on the evening news with my gold tooth hitting off those camera lenses! Speaking truth like my two sistahs!

Just call me Sassy, aka Sassafras.

Maybe I could have been a world-class athlete.

I watched Flo Jo Joyner during the Olympics back in '84.

"*I can do that if I had the right spot trainer,*" I thought to myself.

When I got half-way around the track, I fell, rolled out of my lane, and took out two other runners.

And I fainted if I am in the sun too long.

Now, I just sit and watch Wide World of Sports in my air-conditioned apartment sipping on Canada Dry mixed with Gatorade.

Just call me Sassy, aka Sassafras.

Maybe I could have been a docile housewife like Florida on the show "Good Times."

But I'm no ectomorph-type Olive Oyl looking for a Mr. Popeye!

"Ain't no kid going to sass me, and no baby daddy push up on me. I will take a skillet and bust his head down to the gristle. I am as free as a plastic whistle made in China hidden in a box of Cracker Jacks."

Just call me Sassy, aka Sassafras.

Maybe I could have been an opera diva!

I once saw Jesse Newman when my music class went to New York.

When she slung those high notes, I chased after them, too.

But I sounded like a banshee gagging on a catfish bone.

My grandma suggested that I drink Pepsi the next time I try to sing. It would loosen the vocal cords.

But I don't like Pepsi. Too strong. I might try a Coke!

Just call me Sassy, aka Sassafras.

Maybe I could have been a poet laureate!

I love Nikki Giovanni!

As Langston Hughes once said, "*She wouldn't take no tea for a fever!*"

In college, she majored in Fine Arts but minored in the "black arts." She was heavy into protesting during the 1960s Civil Rights Movement!

She spent many of her radical days carrying a protest sign and writing poetry about what she saw, felt, and heard.

Like Nikki said, "*I don't want to brag and indeed not boast. But you can't take anything from me but notes!*"

When I take walks, I talk to myself because I'm the smartest person I know, and the only one I trust. I love smelling the dust on a dirt road just before it rains. I love taking long walks and reciting the poetry I read. But you can best believe I will be home before mama steps out on the porch and hollers my legal name for the whole county to hear.

Just call me Sassy, aka Sassafras.

She is who I am and who I shall remain!

*Dedicated to Patricia June, my sister

Karen's Klownitis!

Child, I can't catch my breath or rest my eyes
So light-headed and dizzy from Karen's lies
Threaten to call in back-up if I cough or sneeze
All up in my face, though she's the one uneased

Stood on my property, refused to move aside
Called me racist names contempt she couldn't hide
How dare I even breathe, laugh, or be amazed
While Ms. Karen acts a tab bit crazed

Bi-polar is on overload suspect she missed her meds
Instead of offering sympathy, I leaned to her instead
"I know you are afraid, so I'll keep my dignity
The furthest thing from my mind is to react ignorantly

I will keep this short, give you a piece of advice
Don't run up on a sister. Some aren't very nice
If you bum-rush a black queen, who is without her crown
You will find yourself recovering from a relentless beat down"

She said I should be locked up; that I don't have any right
I took one step towards her, like a bird, she took flight
I videotape the drama. I will need proof later on
When the police arrive, they tell her to move along

It took all in me to keep my hands off the broad
After her award-winning act, she 'gazelle' across my yard
I confess I left out the part about releasing the hounds
They nipped her ankles; you should have seen her clown

Kinky Hair

I went on a job interview last Tuesday
Professionally dressed, my hair was slayed
I was on my best behavior and good manners
I arrived extra early, noted on my day planner

One of two finalists with outstanding credentials
I thought I had it on lock with so much potential
Read a magazine until I heard my name called
I had no idea I was about to meet Neanderthals

When I entered, they gawked at my kinky hair
You should have seen their shock, awe, and stares
Deer in a headlight gaze and gaping mouths
I knew this interview was heading South

I greeted everyone by extending my hand
With a bubbly hello, a child could understand
They avoided my gaze started shuffling papers
One of the panelists caught the vapors

They began with basic questions as if killing time
It felt like an interrogation, like I committed a crime
Never asked about my credentials how I would fit in
More absorbed with hairstyles worn by black women

One asked how often did I wash and comb my tresses
Then went around the table making wild, crazy guesses
Another said, "*twice a month*" as if it was conceivable
They debated my hair's hygiene like I was invisible

I tried to return the interview to its original purpose
A young male leaned over to stroke my hair's surface
I threw up both hands, let out a horrifying gasp
Like a Taekwondo master, I blocked his grasp

The interview terminated. I couldn't wait to leave
A panelist thanked me, grateful for a reprieve
When I left the room, I was instinctively aware
They won't be hiring a sister with kinky hair

*To my sisters who love the natural styles

Mannequin

The first sin recorded poor Eve felt betrayed
Adam told his first lie because he was afraid
Men refuse to see women as intelligent souls
Instead lay on them like a sheet, they unfold

One reason some men treat women second-class
Their sexual thirst is like gulping from a glass
Her body is their map to a lost, hidden treasure
Below the neckline is where they find pleasure

Males think they have a right to degrade females
Slide boney fingers over her like reading braille
Some females are accustomed to being debased
Shown little decency, disfavored or disgraced

He calls her sweetie, honey, a luscious baby doll
He uses profane language when he makes catcalls
Like Jamie stalked in a Halloween movie sequel
Men who select her birth control don't see her as an equal

Some women don't have an opinion about men's perception
Accept the disrespect go along with the deception
She will accept her fate for the sake of survival
Until she finds the inner strength to start a revival

She protests in the streets for women's equal rights
Demands mutual respect from men who act like parasites
Argue Roe vs. Wade rebuked a ban from the Vatican
She came from Adam's side. She's not a mannequin!

Masquerade

Before you leave home and enter a workplace
Apply more than makeup on your face
Change word inflections when you are with others
So, they can't detect the origin of your mother

Make sure your attire and hair don't offend
While you go out of your way to meld or blend
Then try to impress, using complicated words
You're not a screeching owl but a mockingbird

Embarrassed of your race, ethnicity, and African culture
You refused to share your origin, don't feel like a lecture
Never date your color or mix with your kind
Ashamed of your melanin skin, act color blind

History taught you not to acknowledge your heritage
Refuse to research black roots only white relatives
For centuries we have come under vicious attack
Is that why you are unable to relate to blacks?

As much as you would like to imitate the Cleavers
All the money on earth won't make you the Beaver
You're tired of the harassment, being treated like dirt
A bigot won't drink with you; he'd rather die of thirst

No one says you can't befriend people of other races
Just don't get confused believe you're trading places
Get to know your ancestry and your stunning brown skin
Take off your mask; love the skin you're wrapped in

Me, Too

She didn't know what to think. It was just a blind date
First dinner and a movie, would not be out too late
Not the least bit interested but much to her chagrin
Her bestie hounded her, so she finally gave in

They met at a neutral place agreed to take one car
He stares and licks his lips like she's a snack bar
The greeting was awkward; she was not impressed
He acted immaturely, didn't date much, she guessed

Straight out the gate, he rests his arm on her back
Unaware he would later launch his sexual attack
She became impatient, wants to end the charades
Please let this nightmare end; she silently prays

She returns to his home, where he lives with his mom
She heard the warning siren but ignored the alarm
He asked her if she wanted to see his bachelor's lair
She threw caution to the wind, follows him downstairs

He hungrily asked if they could date again
The very sight of him gave her crawling skin
He grabbed her purse and held it from her reach
She just met this man. Now her trust is breached

He tries to kiss and caress her as he had before
Without warning, he drags her across the tiled floor
Then shoves her on a bed that looked like a cot
It was useless to scream no one in earshot

He places two fingers around her throat
Applies intense pressure, she begins to choke
The assault was demeaning and so surreal
She was in a state of shock didn't know what to feel

His facial expression changes to a frightened kid
She is shocked and traumatized by what he did
He drops his head and refuses to look in her face
Did not try to stop her as she fled from his place

Many years have passed since the horrible night
She has PTSD, which became her plight
What gives her hope, though, she lost her virtue
When she hears other victims are crying, "*Me, too!*"

Dedicated to victims of date and workplace rape

Michelle O!

She is such a classy lady with a contagious smile
So regal and elegant, no evidence of guile
Perfect role model, worth her weight in gold
Her kind of woman can't be bought or sold

Michelle L. Robinson-Obama the first Black FLOTUS
A native of Chicago's Southside, America took notice
At Princeton and Harvard Law, she studies to be a lawyer
The law firm of Sidley & Austin was her first employer

Met her husband, Barack Obama, who enthralled her heart
So, in love with this man, they seldom were apart
In pursuit of their dreams, each follows their career
Barack pursued politics, Michelle's path was clear

Both motivated and driven, they made a formidable team
Their aspirations and goals were not a pipe dream
When Barack announced his candidacy for the U.S. President
Michelle hit the campaign trail and spoke at major Party events

A writer, a speaker, an advocate for children's health
Choosing nourishing meals were as vital as one's wealth
Proud of the roles she had but the one she treasures most
Mother of Malia and Sasha, to whom she's hugely close

Since she left the White House with the first black President
Now back in the public's eye needs no one's consent
Authored a book, "*Becoming*" reveals her point of view
There's nothing left to prove what she will or won't do

Keep an eye on the former first lady; don't sleep on this queen
She's the Party's pick-me-up, like a cup of strong caffeine
Only she knows the future or what her next move will be
Like a game of chess, each strategic move charts her history

*A tribute to former First Lady Michelle Obama, FLOTUS

Ms. Maxine!

When did it all begin? What's in Maxine Water's pedigree?
You think she has no bragging rights; let me share her history
Born and raised in Saint Louis, the family moved to LA
Paid her dues in public service, not denied nor delayed

A city councilwoman; member of California's state's assembly
Fought against apartheid for those who sought democracy
Joined the Democratic Party, elected to the U.S. Congress
Debates her colleagues, reclaims her time, refuses to digress

Chaired Congressional Black Caucus, never anyone's token
Marched for civil rights, known to be outspoken
Accused of breaking Party rules, they did not like her methods
She defended her position, don't ever question her ethics

Short and petite in stature, a fool she will not tolerate
If you misquote her, she will set the record straight
She quotes the constitution, believes in its every word
Denounced the GOP and Trump's behavior as being absurd

Supports the Democratic platform stands for what is right
Not one to mince her words will fight with all her might
Her foes think her time is up; she has served too long
Maxine's on cruise control; they couldn't be more wrong

Trump says she's a loudmouth, with an empty message
He engages her in a battle of wits; he crawls from the wreckage
To her political opponents, let me gently warn you all
Don't come for Maxine Waters unless you ready for a brawl

Redd Bone

Hey, fair-skinned sister with the sexy eyes
What is it about you that ebony females despise?
If you were a redbone under the confederate flag
You could be no darker than a brown paper bag

They say, "*The blacker the berry, the sweeter the juice*"
If a redbone's looks are lovely, she can easily seduce
Her hair is straight, kinked, or tightly curled
To a lot of males, she is a coveted trophy girl

Her DNA mingled with black and white seeds
Called high yeller, half-n-half, or mixed breed
The freckles on her face are so prominent
Those reddish undertones are a compliment

With mulatto blood mixed in her genealogy
Those closest to her are her worse adversary
Earned brownie points for her vanilla skin
Ignored or rejected by her dark-skinned kin

During the Movement, she supports her race with a fist
No one took her seriously. At times she felt dissed
If her soft skin is too fair, there's a threat of rejection
It's often difficult for her to fit in or make a connection

They say redbones go through life getting in for free
While brown-skin females have to pay an entrance fee
They say, "*How have you suffered or been denied*
When it comes to your skin shade, doors open wide"

Suffering from intra-racism is incredibly wrong
Ostracizing our mixed-blood folks like they don't belong
We can argue back and forth that colorism exists
But among our people, we need to cease and desist

Reason to Smile

Abandoned by a mama who gave her away
Refuse to love her, treats her like a stray
Roams from pillar to post, desires to belong
No kiss for her lips, no lyrics for her song

A child prodigy, no one knows her name
Anesthetized emotions suppress her shame
Where would she turn while she clings to hope?
How would she survive, how could she cope?

Her country refuses to protect her rights
Faces each new day with old battles to fight
The streets are her home; she covers her face
She looks over her shoulder can't find a safe place

She finds a basement that is cold and dank
No charity for this orphan and no one to thank
Body parts snatched like a cast-off rag doll
She finds the courage to rise whenever she falls

A victim of violent assaults at every turn
Physical abuse from males became a pattern
The abuse was relentless, not a shred of affection
From those who could have offered protection

Among all the chaos, she delivers a boy
He becomes her pride, her heartbeat, her joy
It gave her the strength to stay in the race
She sheds the skin of shame and disgrace

Discovers her muse in the gifts of her hands
Remarkable artwork is known all over the land
Reaches the age of majority, no longer a child
Rises from the ashes with a reason to smile

Ruth, My Ride or Die

Ruth and I were besties; that is what we were
If I needed her to talk to, she was always there
Met when we were youngsters around the age of six
Ruth was Lucy. I was Ethel – we pulled similar tricks

Her comedic sense of humor always made me smile
We had a lot in common, down to our fashion style
We got into trouble. Of course, we had our flaws
But never in competition, forgave our few faux pas

Dancing was our forte, always toned and trim
We were both tall and lean, once called "Virginia Slim"
When we became adults, we were birds of a feather
My ride or die and I faced calm or hostile weather

Thick as thieves, forever in each other's company
Devoted to our friendship, never any rivalry
We double-dated and talked about getting married
I was her maid of honor and god-mom to a boy she carried

Due to our life choices, we followed different paths
Grateful it wasn't the result of a distasteful aftermath
Vowed to stay in touch with calls, emails, or letters
When life got too chaotic, we hoped things would get better

When she told me she was ill; the prognosis wasn't good
I tried to lift her spirits, let her know I understood
As her health declined, she attempted to downplay
How sick she was, we hoped God would make a way

The call finally came from her family to say goodbye
I didn't want to accept that my friend was going to die
Standing by her bed conjuring memories of our past
She exhaled a quiet breath, my best friend to the last

*In memory of Deborah R. Author, my life-long friend (1950-2010)

She Stops, Stares, and Sighs

She is watching a woman, not of her race
Kiss the cheek of a black man's face
She's carrying a racially-mixed child
They express their love. There's nothing to hide
A black woman stops, stares, and sighs

An unscrupulous colleague receives a raise
Basked in all the "well done" praise
Took all the credit and rejected advice
Thieves will steal and don't think twice
A black woman stops, stares, and sighs

Respond to a cattle call. Both get an audition
Theatre casting is a cutthroat competition
Ripe for the role, she pours out her heart
Rival offers sex and wins the part
A black woman stops, stares, and sighs

At promotion time, and she is next in line
Can perform any tasks, a brilliant mind
A job of a lifetime senior vice president
Résumé comes up missing by accident
A black woman stops, stares, and sighs

Accused of being too loud and distracting
Bitter at injustice, always overreacting
Her man says he cheated, but she can't get upset
She wears her hair in braids with a hairnet
A black woman stops, stares, and sighs

Those females from other ethnicities
Hurling insults that sisters are no beauties
An androgynous-looking Sojourner Truth
They are rachet, boisterous and uncouth
A black woman stops, stares, and sighs

Not seen as a loner but part of a crowd
Pretends to be docile; avoids acting proud
Sapphire nor Jemima is her legal name
All angry black women act the same
We're too busy reclaiming our time to stop, stare, and sigh!

She's Listening

When I am on the phone, what I say she hears
Tear down other queens while I conceal my fears
She hears me trashing colleagues or my friends
Teaches my little missy it's alright to pretend

How I treat her dad show him little respect
Prove that I can easily dismantle or dissect
His fragile self-esteem, most of all his dignity
Reveals to her the self-hate that abides in me

I am like Sirius-XM; she tunes in every day
She hears me talk without a filter; I don't care what I say
No empathy for others not sympathetic or kind
Refuse to hold my peace, say what's on my mind

I must teach my child that I have what it takes
Show my mini-me I can correct my mistakes
I want to be the best role model in her world
Always careful that I am handling a pearl

Get along with females who aren't my enemy
No jealousy or resentment should she ever see
Be a loyal and dear friend to those whom I love
Sweetly handle my little angel with kid gloves

Side Piece

He swore up and down she was just his niece
All this time, she was his secret side piece
He kept her hidden on the backside of town
Daddy left a queen to hold a harlot down

We never thought he would abandon our camp
Being seen in public with the town's infamous tramp
I could not understand the type of spell she cast
That would seduce him to abandon us so fast

Dad worked hard at the factory, had plenty of cash
He gave every single penny to that piece of trash
She had a home, a sports car, and a platinum card
Our home looked like Sanford & Son's side yard

The woman seduced Daddy with so many lies
We didn't fault her; it was him we despised
He prided himself on being fast and slick
He spent his free time with an over-the-hill trick

Mama loved that man who once was her king
He was charming, handsome, wore an earring
Casanova showed no interest in his kids or wife
He treated us like dirt while living a pimp's life

Mama once told us Daddy was a notorious flirt
Always in the streets chasing young short skirts
When he deserted her, she would not speak his name
She became a recluse, hiding in her shame

Daddy's spare rib sent word that he died
His back-alley concubine wept at his bedside
No, we didn't mourn him, didn't take it as hard
We still pick at the scabs of our old ugly scars

He broke mama's heart and her will to live
Only for her sake did I even try to forgive
We were all victims of a multi-train wreck
His employer denied "his wife" a survivor's check

It has been years since our Dad deserted us
When I see his photo, I look away in disgust
Living with a married man took some nerve
Ms. Karma made sure they both got served

Sunrise Debut

She comes from the back. Her steps are unsteady
Apparent to everyone, she isn't quite ready
Very lean and tall, her hair looks a mess
And it looks like she slept in her dress

Their minds made up by the judgment of others
"The poor girl can't sing," sighs a church mother
Everyone is whispering; their gaze said it all
She braces herself for their sneers and catcalls

She bows her head; launches into her solo
Her eyes shut tightly; she sings real low
The pastor knew well who the song was about
So, he gently said, *"Child, open your mouth!"*

She ends the first verse and releases a squall
Every high note runs straight up the wall
During the second verse, her octave gets higher
You could hear a pin drop in the mass choir

In the final verse, the first lady rolls under her pew
And asks a poor usher to find her lost shoe
When the soloist hits an E6, the director falls out
The organist shouts, *"That's what I'm talking about!"*

She rips that spiritual from the bottom to top
Everyone is numb; their lower jaws dropped
When she ends her rendition, they can only stare
Old Sam, not strapped in—slid out of his wheelchair

We left the sunrise service and told others the story
At the dawn of the day, an angel ushered in Glory
The lesson we learned but ashamed to discover
Don't ever try to judge a book by its cover

Thick Chicks

We are thick and juicy as prime pork rib
If you want a taste test, please wear a bib
Full volume and opulent, a sight to behold
Men drool like ex-cons released on parole

Every bit of our curvaceous frame is plus-sized
Big-boned, full-figured, and succulent thighs
Large lips, flared nostrils, and sultry brown eyes
Love our high-caloric foods deep-fried

Soul food cooking, we got Madea to thank
To smooth our folds, we wear tummy tuck Spanx®
We dance and flirt. We are so confident
Sweet treats, too many snacks, so indulgent

The fashion designers love our voluptuous girth
Just don't ever dress us like Mrs. Butterworth
Strut catwalks and runways showcasing our stuff
Under our haute couture is a lot of cream puff

Pleasingly plump, we look phat to most men
Have no craving or thirst to be thin as bobby pins
Thighs rubbing together makes the sweetest noise
Way too much woman for the Dallas Cowboys®™

Implants are popular, and we got huge breasts
Guys like a full-grown chest, not a sparrow's nest
We are proud of DD-size cups and double chins
Not trying to Keep up with the Kardashians ®™

We love to set a mood with a room full of candles
It's no sin that men like to grab our love handles
We expose lots of flesh as much as we please
Carrying this extra weight is crushing our knees

Throw Up Both Hands

Arose before the rooster could sound an alarm
Stoked embers in the stove, put a big kettle on
Tried not to wake the family who was still asleep
My man got drunk last night; he snores so deep

Fry two eggs, a slice of fatback, a cup of cornmeal
It would be more than enough to get my fill
I sat down at the table, bowed my head to say grace
Thankful that white trash won't kick us off the place

Caught a fever, took a rag to wipe sweat from my brow
No medicine to help me feel better no how
Hands cracked and scaly from blistering hot water
Can't buy a moisture salve it cost more than a quarter

A chicken farm is worse than picking cotton
Fresh breeze on my warm face long since forgotten
No matter I'm sucking air, and my nose is runny
The owners only care about quotas and money

I tried to finish chores before my ride pulls up
Wash a pot and plate dried my chipped coffee cup
Step out on the porch looking down the road
I kept on begging Jesus to lighten my load

When I was a girl, I dreamt of traveling the world
I wanted to sing, flaunt my shape, sling my pretty curls
Have men buy me ribs, drinks, dress me up, and such
Startled when a rat makes tracks across my dusty hutch

I would live in a palace, like Cinderella bell of the ball
Not a tin-roof shack with newspaper on the walls
I birthed six horrid children with a worthless man
With the strength I have left, I throw up both my hands

Toxic Heart

She allows him in. He punches her in the face
Blood mixed with saliva flies over the place
Her eye begins to swell around the socket
He steps over her and shoves his fist in his pocket

He had been out drinking, which he often did
The fact he was an angry drunk couldn't be hid
If she looked at him wrong, it was on and popping
Unless someone interfered, there was no stopping

A history of violence was a veil of thin film
She had done nothing wrong accept tried to love him
Shouting at the top of his lungs, disturbing the peace
Neighbors intervened, placed calls to the police

Sometimes he would spend one night in jail
The next day she was at the court posting bail
Children were traumatized out of their minds
No one in whom to confide, no sympathy to find

How she suffered him is beyond one's mental scope
Twenty long years, how in the world did she cope
She was sorry she ever married this man
The children were stressed and tired of his rants

Finally, the victimizer fell sick and died
She stopped hiding her pain, swallowed her pride
Domestic violence had torn her dignity apart
She lived out her days nursing a broken heart

We've Come This Far...Still So Far to Go!

Black women have struggled since their birth
Their haters won't agree, but they know their worth
No accomplice, not one to leave the scene of a crime
They get more done in a year than some in a lifetime

Raped by her owner, caused her to bear his seeds
He forced her man to watch no thought of his needs
She suckled the master's baby sang it lullabies
Slave babies went without breast milk and died

Disrespected, demeaned, disqualified, and dismissed
Always in an altercation with those who want to resist
Treated like the calvary expected to come with the fix
"Beulah, bring the mop and bucket clean up on aisle six!"

Cook for everyone while she is on the Daniel fast
The last shall be first, and the first shall be last
The era of Aunt Jemimah and Sapphira is ending
Sisters advancing to the forefront is trending

Doctor, lawyer, judge, and law enforcement
Mayor, congresswomen, senator, CEO, and president
They now have earned an adult seat at the table
Don't try to breastfeed them like they still in a cradle

Though women of color know they have a place in the line
Still support everyone else while they remain behind
McCloud, Truth, Hamer, many who paved the way
Kudos to the caliber of women leading today

Stacey Abrams registers 800K during voter suppression
In time to defeat Trump during the 2020 election
Her leadership and relentless efforts were not in vain
Georgia, you all better put some respect on her name

Mayor Keisha Lance Bottoms gifted Biden her state
Far too long a bloody red, she could not tolerate
Supported Black Lives Matter from Dixie withdrew
Now, Georgia's favorite color is any shade of blue

No surprise Kamala Harris' brain would take her far
An HBCU graduate, AKA, passed the California bar
First female, first black, and South Asian in government
Served as a state senator is now America's vice president

Black women always knew if only given a chance
Proven they could do more than sing or twerk dance
Not booty and boobed bimbos on the arm of a man
Bring home the bacon and heat it in a Teflon pan

They've come this far by faith; there's no turning back
Tired of arguing with rivals that keep talking smack
I hope that you can swim; the Red Sea already split
They are not just living history but rewriting it

Tribute to Vice President-elect Kamala Harris, Community Activist Stacy Abram, and Georgia's Mayor Keisha Lance Bottoms, our trailblazers

When Black Women Gather

When black women gather, we can drop the heat
March three rows deep by our drumbeat
Celebrate a win against the odds; we rejoice
United together, in spirit, lift a single voice

When black women gather to mourn or to travail
About an injustice, loss of a child, or to exhale
Bound by strength and support of what we need
If one of us is wounded, then we all bleed

When black women gather, we refuse to tear down
Another one's character, image, or a crooked crown
We share the same gender, attributes, or emotions
Not catty, petty, or vindictive, only devotion

When black women gather to chit-chat and chew
We conceal negative vibes because we all have issues
Share deep, dark secrets in hopes one will heal
Not spread gossip or hearsay our secrets are sealed

When black women gather to worship and pray
Heaven takes notice knows we don't come to play
God looks into our hearts and hears us when we wail
Reminding us the Gates of Hell will not prevail

As long as black women gather, we will be a success
Hold each other accountable; forget not to bless
Cover and uplift each sister demonstrate real love
Proven wise as serpents; yet, harmless as doves

Tribute to "When Black Women Gather," a private Face book group

Why She Mad?

When you were born, did you get a slap?
Fall on your head from your mama's lap?
Poor Sophia, did you fight all your life?
Exposed to so much toxicity and strife

The family accursed with fiery hot tempers
Regularly spar like lightweight contenders
Way out of control like a thunderous storm
Quick to throw a fit, never try to conform

Full of hot rage, almost foam at the mouth
Don't even care what the topic's about
Lips poked out, so mean and hateful
For once in your life, can you be grateful

Always knew you would clown or perform
So why do you always stray from the norm
Life ends way too soon, and time is too short
Spewing venom from your hateful thoughts

Intimidating others seem to keep you amused
Is the blood in your veins demonically transfused?
Spiteful behavior is something you learned
You will learn today because the tables have turned

Blood pressure is completely off the charts
The stress alone is destroying your heart
One day you will end up blowing a gasket
A young, pretty corpse in a satin-lined casket

Wonder Woman!

As a crusader, you think you're as tough as steel
Hate to break the news, but it's time for the reveal
Hyperventilating as if your heart would burst
Let others cut in line though you were there first

You keep running game on those in the streets
Weep with Atlanta Housewives when men cheat
In your own home, you are under restraints
Men say you're pretty but running low octane

Feel insecure like he's two-timing or untruthful
Chasing skirts since you're no longer youthful
He wants to get married so he can hold you down
There you are across town trying on wedding gowns

Your job is so stressful you haven't been sleeping
Locked away in your room taking selfies or weeping
Everyone gets promoted or receives a pay raise
You so resentful want to set the place ablaze

Try to be everything to everybody causes mental stress
Some get away with murder while you under duress
Females don't like you call you out of your name
Treat you like a guest on the Family Feud Game®™

There is more to you than a cape and vinyl boots
Play dress up or fantasize because the outfit is cute
Wonder woman loves herself who she has become
She is no one's option nor under anyone's thumb

Want to be a woman of steel with a fancy cape
Don't crawl from a brawl looking for an escape
Stand up to your bullies and those who intimidate
Straighten your tiara. Stop trying to accommodate

The enemies you battle are occupying your mind
You fight battle trying to save humankind
Pop your bubble and take your place in the world
You can't be a wonder woman and a frightened girl

SECTION FOUR

BROTHERS' WOOLEN TAPESTRY

An innocent black man in a kangaroo court
I will stand by your side and lend moral support
Trumped-up charges and refuse to acquit
When your enemies die, we will post their obit

A Blue-Collar Bishop

Phillip Thomas hailed from the City of Baltimore
Relocated to Virginia to see what was in store
For him, as he mingled ministry with music
Pursued and panted after God like a narcotic

A marked man, an attempt made on his life at birth
Adversaries tried to block him from entering the earth
While he grew in his silently mama's womb
Instead of a baby crib, the enemy erected a tomb

But his Heavenly Father laid the perfect plan
This seed would grow to be a servant's man
God put a hedge around him kept him secure
He increased in strength as he spiritually matured

Into a worshipper, God said he would one day become
Created a gospel group with friends into a foursome
They agreed *MPRT* would be a good fit
Until God called him to the prophet's pulpit

Behind the sacred desk, his words had a unique sound
"*Where sin abounds, grace did much more abound.*"
Ascended the clerical ranks with others who remained
Elevated to Bishop where he was ceremoniously ordained

As a spiritual overseer to those who were assigned
Sons and daughters who joined were proud to align
Gifts and talents with one they trust had God's favor
Committed to get in the trenches and do the labor

Thomas could be an elitist with prominence and great fame
An impressive list of accolades accompanying his name
Instead, he chooses to serve the forgotten man
With a blue-collar ministry only, his God could plan

*A loving tribute to my pastor, Bishop Phillip O. Thomas,
Pastor of Highview Christian Fellowship, Fairfax, VA*

A Knee on the Neck

George was a black man and assumed a threat
A trip to a convenience store, he would later regret
Selected a few items and chose to pay with change
Pulls out a single bill the cashier viewed as strange

The manager summoned the police to the store
A black man passing a fake bill that he couldn't ignore
George's twenty-dollar bill looked counterfeit
When he first walked in, he did not look legit

Four stormtroopers arrived to arrest this one
Bystanders videotaping knew George had no gun
After everything went down, he sat in his car
When ordered to step out, things went a bit too far

Handcuffed, down on his face, he began to plea
On the base of his neck, one officer applied his knee
George begged and cried; he could not catch his breath
The horseman of the Apocalyptic cared less what he felt

Fifty years ago, James Brown said, "*Say it loud!*"
In this racist country, it's hard for Blacks to be proud
In less than nine minutes, life was gone over an alleged bogus
bill
Not by a hail of bullets but a police officer's boot heel

*In remembrance of George Floyd, a victim of police brutality
on May 25, 2020*

A Man Named John

There was a man named John from a town called Troy
A small rural hamlet in Alabama, a metropolis to a boy
Blessed with a peaceful spirit and love for his fellow man
Preaching came easy when it's part of God's plan

John preached to a brood of chickens his only congregants
Protective of his flock, he would defiantly defend
Joined the Civil Rights Movement to instigate good trouble
Fought for voters' rights, his mouth racists couldn't muzzle

Selma, Montgomery, and Nashville vilified demonic strongholds
Black men and women arrested; the world saw it unfold
John and his comrades faced death threats and relentless
violence
King, Lawson, Vivian, Nash, Lowry, others bore it in silence

As SNCC Chairman, the jails he would often inhabit
A racist law enforcement system failed to break his spirit
Quiet and bashful, yet; his words were loud and clear
Led from the front or brought up the rear without fear

Over thirty years, John served in Congress, a lamb in a lion's
lair
Unless on a mission, seldom absent from his elected chair
Colleagues knew his life's work, watched requests denied
On the Voting Rights Advancement Act, his name shall be
applied

Who knew this peaceful warrior would one day be so loved?
Admired for his courageous heart and shedding his blood
No matter who crossed his path, he treated all the same
We plan to gather at the bridge that will one day bear his name

In memory of the late Congressman John L. Lewis (GA)

Black Lives Do Matter

They say that our talk is just chatter
If we demand that Black lives do matter
Men and women denied civil rights
Most are victims of senseless gunfights

Get stopped for almost any reason
Shot down as an act of high treason
By a few self-proclaimed racist cops
Their excuse, a routine traffic stop

With hands raised still under attack
Even worse will get shot in the back
Cast aside like a piece of spoiled meat
Left to die like a dog in the street

Racist supporters don't want police tried
No surprise prosecutors have lied
Loud protests bring no legal support
Too much leniency in the courts

Laws refuse to protect our black men
When a fixed fight is hard to win
They've been labeled immoral and vile
Not seen as a black mother's child

Mothers want it to be understood
Let their young men enjoy adulthood
They are tired of the smoking guns
That keep taking the lives of their sons

We must march to bring about peace
Pray all of this violence will cease
Protesters still vent their frustration
Aren't we still a civilized nation?

In memory of minority victims of police brutality

Buffalo Soldiers

From the South, they walked or rode on horseback
Freed slaves joined the Army to take up the slack
Training those who were illiterate was a daunting task
A chance to serve their country was all they asked

The blacks assigned to the 9th and 10th cavalry regiment
Took an oath to serve and defend was to their detriment
An honorable nickname that the Indians bestowed
Due to their tight curly mane resembling a buffalo

Some were run-a-way slaves who desired to be free
Hunted by bounty hunters who charged a nominal fee
Return them to the plantations to work until they died
The Fugitive Slaves Act claimed they were justified

Thousands of Indians lost their lives, at the brink of extinction
General Custer hailed a hero received an honorable mention
Buffalo soldiers played a role in driving Indians from the West
While back home, slaves were lynched and sent to their death

Their paltry pay was no more than nickels and dimes
Dereliction of their duties was equal to war crimes
Fought in many Indian battles; yet, heroes they became
Some lost their land in Tulsa to which a few held claims

Sent for overseas deployment until World War Two
Overlooked for recognition accolades long overdue
Despite racism and injustice, they're a part of our history
Memorialized for their exploits beyond the call of duty

Did Ms. Amy Cry Real Tears?

Ms. Amy watched a black man as he observed some birds
Blacks are so unpleasant is what she often heard
Though she ignored a leash law posted by Central Park
As he approached her, she made a snide remark

Who does he think he is? Making a fuss about her unleashed pet
She will teach him a lesson that he won't soon forget
He dared to confront a white woman about her puppy's leash
She whipped out her cellphone and summoned the police

Ms. Amy played her white race card to request a service
"Come lean on a black man who is making me nervous!"
Careful to exaggerate that he's enormous and intimidating
"No, I am not overreacting or discriminating!"

He had the sense to video her antics as she acted out
She's now in his face; her voice raised to a shout
Waiting for the police, she yanked her dog by its collar
Dangled it like a yo-yo as she screamed and hollered

A car finally arrives to get both versions of the story
They thought Ms. Amy's tale sounded like an allegory
She lost her job due to a false report cried bitter tears
The police took the canine, which she claims to revere

Some advice to instigators, please don't play that game
Call 9-11 on black folks so that you can point blame
Use your common sense; don't try to hunt and peck
You may find yourself requesting an unemployment check

Game Changers

The Negro Baseball League was a beast with a bat and ball
A time when negroes weren't worth noticing at all
Put up roadblocks and obstacles petitioning courts
Vowed to keep America's pastime a white-only sport

Negroes kept out of the majors for over forty years
Their prowess of the game was made very clear
Treated as unworthy by their white colleagues
Formed their enterprise, the American Negro League

Wages were low, but the game kept them competing
They played under adversity until their league was fleeting
Not one single white endorsement played with no fame
Birth from their loins were famous names in the game

Josh Gibson's hits made a hardball fly up a hill
Satchel Paige pitched a ball that appeared the skin would peel
In 1947, Robinson broke rank to swim in the white shark's tank
Paved the way for other players like Hank Aaron and Ernie
Banks

Sliding home, stolen bases, pitched a ball like a lightning rod
Notable black ballplayers achieved dreams against the odds
Some played past their prime didn't thaw their determination
Proved they could play baseball despite racial discrimination

In memory of my deceased brother, James June

119

"On December 17, 2020, Major League Baseball welcomed the Negro Leagues into their organization and will integrate statistics and records from seven professional Negro Leagues that operated from 1920-1948 and include approximately 3,400 players as part of its history."

I Got You!

When you leave our home and are under attack
For better or worse, your queen has your back
Meet those who will lie, cheat, kill, and steal
Like a handler does a bronco to break its will

So vile and hateful will call you out your name
Try their best to abort or disrupt your game
Block each door to your golden opportunity
Make your life pure hell, offer no immunity

Refuse to accept your ideas or your honest opinion
Under no circumstances allow you take dominion
Trash your name like dirt; think you are a fool
God promised he would make them your footstool

An innocent black man in a kangaroo court
I will stand by your side and lend moral support
They will offer trumped-up charges refuse to acquit
When your enemies die, we will post their obit

Guard our throne when you are away fighting jackals
I will give up the seat of power when you return to our castle
Comfort you and be there to massage your ego
Lay your head on my breast let your bitter tears flow

SpareMyLife.Com

He's been wrongly accused and is locked up in jail
Sitting on death row for a crime he did not commit
Found guilty of murder, he pleads but to no avail
Even when the real perpetrator finally admits

Someone claims they saw him at the scene of the crime
He works the night shift and was waiting for a bus
His only guilt was being in the wrong place at the wrong time
Prior run-ins with the law, there was no one to trust

They did not find his DNA or one reliable witness
No police cams or Johnny Law to plant false evidence
On his way to spend an evening with his mistress
He admits he was in the area; it was just a coincidence

The Justice Department railroaded many of our black men
No money or support to help them get the best legal defense
They can free him in a heartbeat with the stroke of a pen
His incompetent public defender with a lackluster offense

As the clock ticks down and the appeals stack up unanswered
He sits and waits for the execution date he knows will come
The governor won't respond. They are ready to drop the
hammer
If he does not get a pardon, his veins will taste the venom

*To those falsely accused or imprisoned for a crime they did not
commit

Step in the Right Direction

Stumbled over both feet running straight to sin
No enemy chased me except the one within
The world offered me fresh milk and sweet honey
I thought long and hard about how to get my money

I was born wealthy with a .925 silver spoon
A trust fund baby, father an oil tycoon
I refused to wait for what would come to me
Demanded my inheritance immediately

I begged and pleaded even told a little lie
Father knew the real reason; reluctantly complied
Gave me my birthright along with a long speech
I had no choice but to listen; I'd soon be out of reach

I left my father's home arrogant and grown
Like a fool, I got duped out of everything I owned
Within a year, I wasted every last dime
Made poor choices left with nothing but time

Drugs, women, and alcohol shameful memories
When the smoke cleared, no one was standing but me
I stayed far too long in the lower valley
Slept under cold bridges and in trashy dark alleys

Homeless and forgotten, living on my own
A voice inside said, "*You can always go home*"
One step after another, tears rolled down my face
Prayed my father would forgive my disgrace

Had I listened to him and not chased the streets
I would have chosen another pathway in a heartbeat
There's a way to discern between right and wrong
My dignity was gone, but his love never withdrawn

I made up my mind to seek my father's presence
Ask him to reinstate me by showing reverence
He saw me coming from afar; his arms extended
My oldest brother disagreed; not what he intended

Angry and bitter, he demanded father send me away
One thing father taught when a lamb goes astray
You find it and make sure it is safe and warm
Return it to the fold tucked under your arms

I am grateful for how he demonstrated his love
As it is with our heavenly Father above
One life is no less valuable; that's why Jesus died
Reunited with my Father is how we reconciled

Thanks for Nothing!

Thanks for leaving and not believing in me
Poured me down the drain like a cup of weak tea
You got caught cheating; it wasn't too hard
When you called it quits, it didn't catch me off guard

Thank you for being the one that got away
I would not know peace had you decided to stay
The tension was thick you could cut it with a knife
When you left for good, I came back to life

I'll be the first to admit I didn't always feel like this
The first year or two was a glimpse of bliss
There were a few instances that made me cry
Like when you slid out without a dignified good-bye

I decided rather than be bitter; I would get better
So, I shared a copy of your Dear John letter
That focused on the faults you spitefully pointed out
To my ace dog, gave him something to laugh about

Relieved there was never any physical violence
But my setback was an event, not a death sentence
No longer defined by you nor our shared past
You were not my alpha or omega, first or last

There's no need to worry whether you would return
Having second thoughts is no longer my concern
The love I now cherish is like Fort Knox gold reserve
I do wish you the happiness you think you deserve

The Butler Did It

Worked in public service was their chosen path
Not your garden variety of White House staff
Traveled to Washington, DC from the Jim Crow South
Their eyes wide open but kept a closed mouth

Committed to their calling, worked behind the scenes
Shoes spit-shine polished tailored suits dry cleaned
Stood at attention like boot camp Marines
Rhythmic perfection with synchronized routines

Confined to a lower level where they dwelled
Sun up to sun down, they serve the POTUS well
From the West Wing to the East Wing, they honed their craft
Reaped their boss's praises or his unbridled wrath

They worked the private quarters on the second floor
Punctual, hardworking, but often ignored
The staff's watchword was always devotion
Overlooked when white colleagues got promotions

During their off-time, they always stayed below
Looked down on as a domestic or a house negro
Taunted by their race as fancy-dressed misfits
Some were called Uncle Tom or Stepin Fetchit

Every term of office, they made their presence known
Created a small clique that took care of their own
An elite class of attendants their pride preserved
Earned a spot in history that they each deserved

*To all the African-American men who served as white house
butlers.*

The First Million Man March

1995-2020

Whites hoped the Million Man March would not happen
Black men too intellectually impotent or emotionally barren
Martin and Malcolm dead. There were no more heroes
Jackson and Sharpton viewed as mediocre negroes

America, your words were lies. Back in 1995, you lost big
Those who chose to attend knew they weren't guinea pigs
Converged on the U.S. Capitol for a day of atonement
Over a million men came to reconcile and repent

Didn't take off from work for a funeral or wedding
Brothers confessed to healing and truth-telling
Black kings of a mighty Diaspora in full attendance
Faces set like flint and a warrior countenance

From urban cities and rural towns, all for one, one for all
Shoulder to shoulder across the country heeding a clarion call
From historically black colleges to Ivy League schools
Airplanes, trains, buses, cars and some traveled in vanpools

Every walk of life from Wall Street and from off the corner
Several generations which no man could number
The Honorable Minister Louis Farrakhan gave the keynote
Shared facts about their slavery; what old Willie Lynch wrote

Many admitted to their flaws; some lacked self-respect
Neglected wives and family, their minds dissected
Revealed negative behaviors towards their brothers
Confessed their defiance was a detriment to others

They atoned, reconciled for every sin of commission
Came to heal their minds of a combative condition
Divulge to each other the mistakes they had done
Sit down with white America to quell racial tension

Gain wisdom and knowledge, the power of their skin
Return to the God of their birth connect with all men
Give honor to the ancestors who were their first masters
Confront domestic enemies to avoid imminent disaster

Return to their communities and regain their lost identity
Take their rightful place and rule from a throne of royalty
Respect and defend all females, treat them like queens
Protect their seeds and support them by any means

The men's march was a massive success in many ways
Let's hope their pledges to improve won't just be a faze
Use their power of influence to elevate their race
Dispel ugly stereotypes linked to the black man's face

Tuskegee Airmen - Our Black Ravens

Above the majestic Dolomites and European soil, they flew
World War II flyboys, members of an elitist crew
First of African descent deemed acceptable as aviators
Escort B-17 heavy bomber planes. They were expert navigators

Alabama's Tuskegee Institute, hand-chosen by the Army Air
Force
Precise piloting and formation never veered off course
College fraternity brothers served in a negro-only troupe
Cherry-picked fighter pilots of the 332nd Fighter's Group

Flew beneath the heavens not a fearful one among them
Kept Nazi prey in their crosshairs judged and condemned
P-51 Red Tail Mustangs left Luftwaffe in a fiery path
Decimated the Germans when they provoked their wrath

The squadrons proficiency and efficiency could've flown
blindfold
Opened space for allied bombers to destroy Nazi strongholds
While engaged in daring dogfights with their adversary
In the States, racism raged, committing evil acts and atrocities

Some perished as their mangled planes spiraled down
Fallen black ravens' wings clipped over unoccupied towns
We revere, honor, and salute the Tuskegee Airmen
Their audacious exploits made them true champions

A tribute to the African American men who served as Tuskegee Airmen during WW2

Were My Chains Not Enough?

Brought here in heavy irons from feet to head
If I escaped, would haul me back, alive or dead
Stole my dignity along with my family name
No human should have to endure this much shame

There was a booming market for locksmiths
Forcing slaves to wear cold irons was not a myth
Chains on my feet and waist never entangled
The heaviest strand around my neck would dangle

Their chains were their bigotry, racism, and hate
Counting each link took my mind off the weight
One worn around the waist maimed my spine
A dismal sound when shifting kept me confined

No way were irons seen as a fashion statement
If you got free; there would be a replacement
Bound with these irons was not my choice
Each link spent my strength and silenced my voice

From sun up to sundown, forced to wear ankle shackles
Fighting for my freedom was a constant battle
Tethered like a wild beast to a stall every night
They clipped my wings so I couldn't take flight

Finally granted the freedom, I so desperately craved
From white taskmasters who were vile and depraved
Descendants wear ankle bracelets, waist chains, and handcuffs
When will our people say enough is enough?

Why I Kneel

The national anthem plays. I get down on one knee
My form of protest is a silent plea
It has nothing to do with a veteran's pride
But reveals the frustration I feel inside

Your anthem sounds a lot like white noise
America is not Babylon. We aren't the Hebrew boys
I do respect all veterans, proud of their service
I only want change, but politicians get nervous

You think the only thing blacks did was work on plantations
They were in every significant war defending this nation
Ignore the simple fact that blacks fought on foreign soil
To protect a white man's freedom made their spilled blood boil

Our race is more patriotic than Trump will ever be
In Vietnam, Korea, Iraq, Afghanistan, Africa, Germany
Asleep in Pearl Harbor when the Japanese came to visit
With nothing but a toe tag and body bag as their only exit

Returned from every battle without honor and recognition
Ignored as if they never made a significant contribution
Martin L. King let quiet marches, but still, he died
You prefer to believe Trump. And we know he lied

If I acted like the Panthers coming after your sons
The FBI would take my freedom and every one of my guns
I choose the NFL to protest, but you call it foul
I'm Colin Kaepernick, not General Colin Powell

My protest has nothing to do with American vets
I will stay down on my knee, having no regrets
When racist police stop killing us without a second thought
It won't matter to you where I was when I fought

*Tribute to Colin Kaepernick, a former quarterback of the NFL
who was banned from the league in 2016 because he protested
police brutality by kneeling during the national anthem*

SECTION FIVE

YOUNG FOLKS' ECCENTRIC TAPESTRY

What will the law do to return those lost souls?
Find a way to protect our innocent must be the goal
They are rounding up sex traffickers across the Nation
We must stop pedophiles from stealing a whole generation

A Student's Eyewitness Account

While on my way to school, I stressed about a test
I didn't take time to study but planned to do my best
I thought of skipping class, but this one is Statistics
Dad warned me if I failed, he would go ballistic

To my surprise, I aced it, acting on a hunch
The morning passes fast, to the cafeteria for lunch
I stopped by my locker to get my basketball
Bounced down the stairs, heard trouble in the halls

There's a loud explosion, sounds like a nuclear war
Screams from my classmates cut me to the core
Voices shouting, *"there's a shooter on the loose!"*
Every exit is blocked, I think, what's the use

A lone wolf sets it off; chaos was everywhere
Peace turns into a panic; everyone running scared
Teacher screaming orders to students in her class
They hit the floor to avoid the flying glass

We can hear a male voice shouting obscenities
I hide in a closet with three as scared as me
A teacher shouts to a student to call 9-11
Inform them there's a shooter with a loaded gun

A SWAT team rushes in, flying bullets exchanged
The body count in double digits, a shooter is deranged
Everyone is traumatized. Many staff and students died
Here they come with thoughts and prayers; tired of the lies

Dealing with our grief and raw emotions help us to vent
Traveled to the White House to meet with the President
Enforce stricter background checks so we can all survive
Ban weapons of destruction would go far to keep us alive

*Dedicated to victims of mass public shootings

Badges, Bullets, and Bullies

A cop is in my face brandishing his shield
Pinned down on a squad car against my will
So close, I can read his badge number clear
He can see I am afraid and smells my fear

He smiles with a smirk and a glee in his eye
I knew if things went south, I could surely die
I kept my mouth shut, staring straight ahead
I imagined a call to mother informing her I was dead

His gun was cocked and ready, full with six rounds
No need to try to flex; I was already down
He puts his gun to my head pulls back the trigger
"If you even cough or sneeze, I will ice you n*****"

The weakest ones are often bullies who hide behind their disdain
Spray you like roaches while you are restrained
Claim to fear for their lives when it's four to one
They got no issue with my life. I'm somebody's son

I Wish My Students Knew

When the school term opens, I am ready for class
Creating a curriculum each child can pass
My goal is to spend time inspiring young learners
Put my personal life on autopilot or the back burner

Spend late hours on my laptop writing plans for review
I wish you knew how hard I work; it is my gift to you
On holidays and weekends, going over lesson plans
I promise as your teacher; I will do the best I can

Help you grasp TEAM's virtual learning, how it applies
Please don't forget your password; it identifies
Your access to class assignments and how well you do
How you follow instructions will be up to you

My primary objective is to make sure students thrive
Many sacrifices I have made to build upon your lives
In my nightly prayers, I ask God to meet your needs
When you are out of sight, work hard to succeed

Tackling difficult subjects like how to multiply
You must master this level so that you can qualify
To advance to division, more complex mathematics
Be proud of your efforts; make it seem like magic

Another goal as a teacher is to make your life better
Analyze subject curriculum follow it to the letter
Your attitude creates your success, and how well you think
I can give you water, but I can't make you drink

Work closely with your family to prepare you for tests
My hope by school's end, you will have done your best
If you have any problems; we'll work through them together
When you leave my class, you'll be my students forever

During this pandemic, with each of you in mind
If you apply yourself, you won't be left behind
Your progress is my challenge. I wish you knew
How committed I am and how hard I work for you

Dedicated to all the educators who perform virtual teaching during the COVID-19 pandemic

Jax and Some Mo' Stuff

In the 20th-century how we stayed occupied
During the summer recess, with the books aside
Rushed out of the house while there was still daylight
Met up at the playground out of our parents' sight

Two rules we obeyed and religiously enforced
You must arrive on time and no cheating at sports
Jacks, basketball, hula hoop, and a large hemp rope
Drawing hopscotch blocks with a piece of used soap

Kids from every street would show up by the dozens
Siblings, bullies, ride or die, even visiting cousins
Parents never fretted or had a reason to worry
If a fight broke out; they would come in a hurry

The younger boys shot marbles or traded baseball cards
The girls jumped double Dutch in an adjacent yard
We chose roller-skating when the blacktop was clear
Those pros could somersault without any headgear

We juggled several games to maximize the time
The most favorite games chosen were the prime
Kickball, Red Light-Green Light, and, of course, Tag
Reserved the field for softball and four tattered bags

Shouts grew to a crescendo couldn't identify voices
At nightfall, we chose Simon Says one of the best choices
Generation Alpha mock our games, calling them Jurassic
Today, they love to play what is known as the classics

NRA Sends Thoughts and Prayers

If the NRA wants to offer their thoughts and prayers
    Don't get upset despite the current state of affairs
    It's not their thoughts and prayers are insincere
    Although a polite gesture; we don't care to hear

As card-carrying members, we protect our guns
From our great granddaddies to our great-grandsons
    Those born with a silver spoon to the dixie cups
    From the rich to rural, we refuse to give guns up

The second amendment states we can keep our arms
We will fight you tooth and nail and may do some harm
    The amendment also states we can defend our home
    The law needs fixing, but leave our guns alone

Experienced gun owners only hunt for game
It's not our fault if sociopaths want a glimpse of fame
    We also use firearms for recreational sports
    Your worthless petitions will die a slow death in court

Our hearts go out to the families who see the body count
    But what we spend on firearms is a hefty amount
    The NRA feels your deep pain and may pretend to care
No skin off our noses if they send thoughts and prayers

Read Me a Bedtime Story

Read me a bedtime story, not a fairytale
Hunting season ended on innocent black males
A story to help me sleep so I won't have a nightmare
Just a simple story without too much fanfare

Where mama and daddy can go to sleep each night
Hoping I won't be a victim of a senseless gunfight
By the one who swore to defend and protect
Nor see me on the news with a knee on my neck

Harassment stops, abuse ends, and the killings too
Make an honest truce with the officers in blue
I shouldn't live my life looking over my shoulder
When police feel entitled, their actions are bolder

Give us a chance to become senior men
A chance to enjoy longevity to live out our end
Don't say our life dreams must now be pending
Is there just one narrative with a happy ending?

Ripe or Rotten - First Fruits

Our children only have one chance to be
A result of good rearing in this society
Parents should always teach what is right
Set a bar for what fruitfulness looks like

The home was full of violence and rage
Barely survived a dysfunctional stage
House in chaos. Parents abuse alcohol
Police always responding to 9-11 calls

Now your junior is acting brass and bold
In the home or public, he's out of control
Kicked out of school due to his disrespect
Parents lose custody based on passive neglect

Brought up with genuine concern for others
Be an example for sisters and brothers
Known by all to be an empathetic child
Always makes an effort to go that extra mile

Youngest boy arrives home without his shoes
Your first reaction he was physically abused
Gave a homeless man his "Tims" and sweater
It shows his charitable spirit is beyond measure

You thought it was popular to be a bully
Instigating your sadistic brand of cruelty
Coaxed others to follow like a sect or cult
Physical injuries escalated with each assault

Your daughter leads a wolf pack now
Stalks the weak and frail always on the prowl
She's fixated on getting them in her crosshairs
Like a spider traps an insect inside a snare

Most children take notice or pay attention
How we treat one another and our intentions
Observe every single thing we demonstrate
Whose behavior do you think they will emulate?

Snatch and Grab

I saw on the news snatches and grabs
Little girls turned into harlots like Rehab
Vans lurk at corners in the middle of the day
Snatch and grab those who are easy prey

Runaways want to be out on their own
Won't obey, always threatening to leave home
Acting defiant believe they have become
Smart enough to outwit the predatory scum

Thirteen-year-old texting always on her phone
A driver pulls up when he sees she's alone
Stands at the curb for a scheduled school bus
She was in plain sight; now a mist like a pixie dust

Harvest organs from those victims selected
Worth more dead than alive, their organs dissected
Like a fog suspended over a dark river
Selling body parts, hearts, kidneys, and livers

We hear on the news young people are kidnapped
Carried from state to state in a motorized trap
Not safe in the comfort of a secured environment
Tied and gagged in a damp, moldy basement

What will the law do to return those lost souls?
Find a way to protect our innocent must be the goal
They are rounding up sex traffickers across the Nation
We must stop pedophiles from stealing a whole generation

The Streets

It's midnight. Do you know where your teens are?
Hanging in the streets, sneaking into adult bars
Too old to be at home when the street lights are on
No longer children but still aren't fully-grown

Your seventeen-year-old son tries to be tough
Ventures into gang territory known to be rough
He refuses to obey rules when you beg him to
He prefers to hang out with thugs with no curfew

Your fourteen-year-old daughter is too fresh
Date full-grown men who abuse her flesh
Demons, witches, and warlocks are what she'll find
Sample meth, coke, and crack that alters her mind

Streets beat them down and show no grace
Eat them up, spit them out, not leave a trace
Youth search for attention in empty places
Into the arms of those with deadly embraces

Parents feel helpless but do all they can do
Teens run away, can't stick to them like glue
Children meet predators on chatlines; so mesmerized
Snatched from the playpen by those who terrorize

Thou Shall Not Steal

As kids, we loved being raised by a village
No one's fruit trees were off-limits to pillage
Try as they might, they couldn't keep us from their trees
We climbed to the top, destroyed fruit, limbs, and leaves

The most popular were peaches, cherries, apples, and melons
We ate until we were content and stomachs swollen
Rarely got caught, stole fruits that made the grade
Then off to the playground or a nap in the shade

If we were caught in the act, no need to resist
Punished by the owners, though we did persist
Hard to dodge a scolding when your cover's blown
One by the owner, the worse waiting at home

Stealing fruit was wrong, a lesson hard to learn
Waiting for fruit to ripen was not our concern
We now know it's better to give than to receive
You have to admit; we were some fierce fruit thieves

Trayvon's Tragedy – Part 1 of 3

Walking from a store one night
No clue he would have to fight
A vigilante and a racist guy
Refused to let a young boy by

Challenged to explain his case
All because of his black face
And the fact he wore a hood
Profiled and misunderstood

Now viewed as a black suspect
Life and limb, he would protect
His inner voice told him to run
The pace was no match for a gun

Whose body is lying on the lawn
A young boy by the name of Trayvon
Zimmerman claimed self-defense
Attempts to cover his offense

Mark O'Mara and Don West
Would try to do their level best
A can of tea, a bag of Skittles®™
Jury hands down an acquittal

Now the world is up in arms
Black boys won't be safe from harm
Due to court antics, the case derailed
In the streets, justice will prevail

Trayvon's Travesty - Part 2 of 3

Disturbing facts were hard to follow
Most were difficult to swallow
Judge allows then tosses out
Beyond the shadow of a doubt

Attorney West hits all-time low
The trial's a Roy and Siegfried show
Defense's tactics hard to take
Insults causing hearts to break

Sadly, they listened to both sides
Mounting anger won't subside
The prosecution's case was weak
More like a game of hide-n-seek

An appalling verdict returned
The panel of six has adjourned
Trial's results cause a divide
The government will now decide

State of confusion and unrest
The public seeks a pound of flesh
Complete and utter travesty
Right the wrong of a tragedy

Trayvon's Tribute - Part 3 of 3

Wives of Sanford City all agree
Let George Zimmerman go free
Took the message to the streets
We will not take this as defeat

The public's battle cry is loud
See the numbers in the crowds
Many have joined in the fray
Some boycott while others pray

The racists now are overjoyed
It's open season on black boys
Needless deaths will now abound
Their excuse just stand-your-ground

No matter what the country feels
"Line in the sand" won't be repealed
But we won't give up this fight
Fought too hard for civil rights

Joined the march to share our plight
When they ignored our human rights
All those before us taught us well
Don't stop ringing freedom's bell!

Trayvon's death won't be in vain
Because we have too much to gain
A tribute to every black man
Will not run but take a stand

Who Cries for Me?

As I look out a window at the streets below
See tracks of footprints in the snow
People rushing to their destination
I quietly recall an old molestation

These days young girls and boys never knew
We were up for sale, snatched in plain view
Taken from the corners sold to the highest bidder
Into the arms of a predator hand-delivered

Child molesters lived in our neighborhood
Lusty appetite for girls who were chaste and good
Girls may be fresh as dishwater were still juveniles
No clue those who stalked them were pedophiles

One close neighbor who was known to the family
Watched me like ripe fruit dangling from a tree
He once said, "*You're different from the others*"
Stroked my arm but kept an eye on my mother

He touched my young thigh under my dress
He didn't go too far; I was a work in progress
Swore he'd never tell, said it would be like magic
He crossed the line and too far almost turned tragic

I never told my parents that he touched my flesh
Mama would have fainted, and Daddy under arrest
For assault and battery of a long-time friend
Thankful I was old enough to comprehend

I was innocent and naive of his deviant deflection
But I kept a distance from his vile affection
I could hear mama say what he tried was a sin
He didn't get a second chance to try it again

When I see the news of missing and exploited kids
The youth spent in bondage and slavery God forbid
I came close to losing my virtue and virginity
By a black-hearted villain who would not cry for me

*Dedicated to victims of child abuse, exploitation, and sex-trafficking

SECTION SIX

COMMON FOLK & ORDINARY PEOPLES' COPTIC TAPESTRY

No matter if my poetry is widely read
Praised by the living or forgotten by the dead
Whether my words are condemned or famed
Let them not contradict this poet's good name

A Poet's Prayer

Help me create spellbound ink
Inspire poet lovers to think
Words make one ponder or convey
A menagerie of idioms I portray

Free my mind from writer's block
A vivid imagination to unlock
A poetic rendition one of a kind
Conceived in secret within my mind

Words awaken a rhythmic repartee
Poetically uttered in a soulful soliloquy
Expressions of delirious content
Or grievous with a sad lament

Words conjure levels of pleasure
Seductive beyond measure
Lines exhibit a pattern or rhyme
With a measured cadence each time

Phrases as pure as my soul can abide
Releases a treasure buried inside
Free verse is expressive and notable
Synonyms shared in divine oracles

A turn of phrase divulges emotions
Put pen to paper words unspoken
Germinated seeds of creative ideas
Itching ears are inclined to hear

Absent of distasteful judgment
Words don't conjure up evil intent
Mystical images unable to hide
Avoid plagiarism reveals I lied

No matter if my poetry is widely read
Praised by the living or forgotten by the dead
Whether my words are condemned or famed
Let them not contradict this poet's good name

Black Face

There's this ugly tradition of wearing blackface
Racists act oblivious don't see it as a disgrace
It is disturbing to insult one's dark complexion
How would they feel if we mocked their reflection?

Stereotypes aren't new; Hollywood made them so
Their approach to black folks was to hit us low
Al Jolson was famous for painting his face colored
He never had an issue; he used burnt cork above his collar

Professor Rachel Dolezal impersonates a black female
For reasons unknown, she disregards being pale
She serves as a chapter president of the NAACP®
Exposed she was born white after too much publicity

Blackface evokes a painful history we want to overcome
To see our skin color insulted is not ever welcome
If you see it as offensive, want to see this act erased
Throw your greasepaint away, don't dress up in blackface

Depression

Today you are joyous. Tomorrow you are depressed
Next week you're agitated or even oppressed
Depression is a reflection of how you mentally feel
It's time to reach out to Blue Cross and Blue Shield©™

Medicine can control your frequent mood swings
Anti-depressants may not change a thing
Finding the root of the problem helps to resolve
Whether it's genetic or, some chemicals involved

An incident of sexual abuse or some trauma
It sends you into a tailspin of emotional drama
The smallest thing makes you incessantly weep
Another cause could be the deprivation of sleep

Everyone seems anxious by the issues they face
Some harboring guilt they cannot erase
Hearing inner voices are hard to confront
Abusing drugs through the point of a shunt

Years of health risks if you ignore any treatment
You will need some answers to your questions
Change your route go in another direction
A medical professional can give suggestions

Do not go it alone. Seek professional help
Futile to ignore this or hide it on a shelf
It won't dissipate because you ignore the signs
Seeking mental wellness should be the bottom line

Don't Forget Our Homeless Vets!

The mist caresses a dim street light
There he stands alone on a quiet night
One block away, two at the most
His countenance is pale as a ghost

Bowed his head like a priest in prayer
He looks asleep, just leaning there
In one spot for nearly an hour
All wet from an evening shower

All ignore him, but he stands unfazed
A lost soul who has seen better days
Folks walk by with hardly a glance
Yet, he patiently awaits his chance

I finally approach; he is in full view
Grimy, hair grayed, and askew
Death row inmate awaiting reprieve
His stench made my stomach heave

Face to face, our gaze exchanged
Ashamed, a man begged for change
Full of pride, but there was no need
His tour over, now one less mouth to feed

What branch of service had he served
A discharge he honorably deserved
Going off to war was not his design
Dodged shrapnel and avoided road mines

Marine who pledged Semper Fi
Airforce jet pilot who always aimed high
Joined the Army to be all he could be
Coast Guard patrolling or Navy at sea

Looked into the eyes of a lost life
Done well with two kids and a wife
Excelled in his rank, top of his game
Now without a home, no fortune or fame

I reached in my purse to pull out a ten
I had second thoughts, so I reach in again
I gave all I had but still felt much regret
The money will never buy self-respect

*Dedicated to all homeless veterans - Thank you for your
service!*

Dream Killer

When dreams turn to nightmares; a few I chose to ignore
Relieved some would never haunt me anymore
Chasing dreams comes with a risk like a lotto
A mega jackpot winning you still might blow

My dreams deferred due to a lack of confidence
No one to block my way. It was my interference
Did not fail to plan but planned to fail
I, alone, allowed my dream train to derail

Some wishes and dreams are too unrealistic
Never share with one who is too pessimistic
Remain quiet while you develop your scheme
You will know the right time to reveal your dream

No genie can rub a lamp make your dream a reality
If it comes to fruition, it depends on your ability
Dreams are like volcanoes, overflow when they erupt
They may evaporate if the dreamer gives up

Final Ascent

When loved ones depart, they pass through a portal
An accursed reality that we are merely mortal
Like a mist, the spirit releases and dissipates
Though we sense it, we won't see it vacate

The spirit will separate from its source
It quietly leaves on its appointed course
The intense pain of death and sorrow remains
No one's seen a spirit unrestrained

No matter the cause of our loved one's death
Aware there's no longer measured breath
A precious breath heave makes its final escape
Remains entombed or buried in the landscape

The passage provokes sadness and grief. It is a ritual
If a decedent knew the Savior, it is spiritual
A loved one is gone, the fullness of their life ends
We do not understand nor can we comprehend

A spirit returns to God who made heaven and earth
The value of a former life no longer has worth
Photos evoke memories that are lost or destroyed
Nothing we do or say can ever fill that empty void

From dust, a body came and to dust it returns
A life honored and celebrated has adjourned
We rest in God's promise we shall see them again
In the presence of the One who rules and reigns

Hall's Hill, Our Home

Bordered by George Mason, Glebe Road, and Lee Highway
A village where black residents worked and played
Culpeper to Emerson numbered streets in between
The descendants of enslaved kings and queens

Boundaries created by a segregated Jim Crow county
Never aware that our properties were worth a bounty
Mt. Salvation, Highview Fellowship, and Calloway
Three spiritual havens where we worship and pray

Hard-working people as good as the country club's elite
Enjoy a simpler life with no outside scrutiny or conceit
White neighbors built a "berlin" wall frequently neglected
County refuses to make repairs our complaints rejected

Proud of the businesses built by our entrepreneurs
Results of hard work not prosperous, but neither poor
Government-level workers lived on every street
Two businesses--Hicks and Allen's--proud of our elite

The civic association always committed and concerned
Conduct regular meetings to keep residents informed
Fought for integration in the campaign for civil rights
Marched on Washington to put an end to racial fights

Students who attended Langston got punished and fair grades
Teachers wasted no time correcting those who disobeyed
When white schools integrated, our parents did not tolerate
Children from our village bullied or treated second-rate

On the playground, there were sports; fights often broke out
Teens danced to R&B music was all we thought about
Young men on the corners singing under the street lights
Kids play Simon Says or Red Light on hot summer nights

Everyone wore fashion styles which were all the rage
Parties attended by anyone over and under drinking age
Patronized Suburban Night or Goolsby's Chocolate City
The county tore down a popular site, which was a pity

Gathered for the Turkey Bowl on Thanksgiving Day
Enjoy a game of flag football; there was seldom a fray
Reminisced about long-forgotten and sad tragedies
Sit with village elders share nostalgic memories

Many died or relocated, parents growing old
Several properties have been torn down or sold
Undergoing gentrification no longer the same
New owners moved in with strange surnames

Look for friends on Facebook to keep in touch
Keep up with relationships that meant so much
No matter where we live, our zip code or time zone
Hall's Hill will forever be our home sweet home

*Tribute to my childhood village

House of Hurt

Do you know anyone who lives in a house of hurt?
Ignores logical advice for what it was worth
No one in this crazy family ever got along
Worked 24/7 to prove each other wrong

The dilapidated house was about to tilt
The water table high; the structure up on stilts
There was never any peace in the neighborhood
Neighbors wanted it relocated back in the woods

The family stayed in a foul, despicable mood
Competed with each other like on family feud
No one ever had a pleasant or unprofane word
Fights spilled into the yard, loud voices were heard

The sheriff summoned to the house every fortnight
Sons hauled off to jail for violent fistfights
Constant abuse instigated from the male spouse
People poked fun named it the "psycho house!"

Rumors the father was committing incest
Impregnated his daughters despite their protest
Their mother refused to intervene or stop the abuse
The girls' promiscuity was her feeble excuse

One of these days, they will move out as planned
We will throw a bar-b-que and hire a live band
The celebration will run for an entire weekend
Tear down the house would be a Godsend

I Do. I Did. I'm Done!

We interrupt this union since we fell out of love
The only interaction is we push and shove
Five years in, we noticed sparks did not remain
What used to be natural has now become restrained

Before God and man, we professed our true love
You were my iron hand; I was your velvet glove
We forsook the world and all of our friends
Not allow any outsiders to divide our blend

Since our wedding day, the romance slid downhill
One by one, standing date nights began to chill
In sickness and in health for better or worse
Words once flowed quickly now seem rehearsed

We gradually allowed everyone to take priority
Go our separate ways without apology
Remember the support from our families
Now, the only thing in common is a divorce decree

Dating outside marriage was against the rules
When we lost respect, the heat quickly cooled
Fidelity and honor replaced with lies and mistrust
Choosing outside lovers as a way to adjust

We no longer spend quality time together
Made bad choices that will haunt us forever
It seems a lifetime ago we stood at the altar as one
Now it is over! I do. I did. I'm done!

I Leave this World Empty

I leave this world empty with nothing in my purse
Carried to a resting place in a slowly driven hearse
I leave this world empty with nothing in my pocket
Bank accounts or designer clothes hanging in a closet

To my offspring, my memories are all I have to leave
Remember the good times, try hard not to grieve
To be chosen as your parent was such a pleasure
The closest thing to earthly wealth I will treasure

To my siblings, I leave love from the depths of my heart
How we looked out for each other was a work of art
To my extended family, there is much I could say
Every time we saw each other; night turned into day

To my friends, cherished times making memories
Every treasured moment helped amass a menagerie
We cried and laughed together, which gave me hope
I saved your notes in those jasmine-scented envelopes

If you were an acquaintance, someone I casually knew
Pleased I had some precious time to spend with you
To a stranger I came upon, I hope we exchanged a smile
And enjoyed each other's company as we talked awhile

To the world, I leave peace for a better tomorrow
My life was well-lived; there's no room for sorrow
I want all my descendants to achieve more than me
So, I leave a doormat inscribed "*be all you can be*"

I, Donald Trump...

Trump stood on the world stage, gave Putin a nod
Fawned over his role model like a demi-god
Trump threw our intel agencies under the bus
The world met his comments with loathing disgust

Kim got the farm when they met in Singapore
Stopped military drills with allies to build rapport
A fan of dictators like murderer Kim Jong-un
He hopes would take nukes off the ground

His party wants him to block colored immigration
Deny anyone entrance from a "s*&^-hole" nation
White evangelicals believe Trump is what we deserve
Are they serious? What kind of God do they serve?

The racists demanded that he turn back the clock
Railed that NFL players were unpatriotic jocks
Reversed most executive orders Obama signed
Revealed his envy and insecure state of mind

He goes around flexing like a bully on a playground
Gave his enemy nicknames, has his base spellbound
To appease them, he tosses out fresh red meat
He keeps tweeting that Democrats went down in defeat

Claimed Mueller's probe was a ball of confusion
Nothing but a witch hunt claiming no collusion
Though his pals found guilty, racking up indictments
He kept the heat on Hillary for his vain excitement

What else can I say about this Thug-in-Chief?
Unable to comprehend a single Intelligence brief
Nothing Putin says or does can be trusted
Trump conspired with Russia; now he's busted

Members of his party tried to lend a voice
Their weak, pathetic words. They made their choice
Won't run for re-election says it's time to move on
Who cares? The GOP signed on as Trump's pawns

He swore on the Bible to defend and protect
A polygraph machine would vehemently object
Be glad when this buffoon is finally off the scene
Passing out irregular pardons like pinto beans

Let Them Eat Corn Cakes!

FLOTUS Melania appears sweet like she might have a heart
People on both sides showed her sympathy from the start
Married to a narcissist who acts just like a child
We hoped her heart was virtuous. We knew Trump's was vile

Immigrated to the states, lied to gain employment
Republicans overlooked it, refused to pass judgment
Brushes Trump's hand away pretends to be defiant
On his money and his name, she is entirely reliant

We watched her on the news, listened to a weak campaign
Struggling to find her voice, instead of finding her brain
Plagiarized Michelle's speech, not one original thought
Her coming out appearance was all for naught

She launched a new slogan let us "*Be Best*"
Spoke against cyberbullies and opioid oppressed
Babies snatched from parents causing hearts to break
Her callous response, "*Let them eat corn cakes*"

She seems to serve no purpose like a ten-cent charm
More like window dressing on her husband's arm
She's quiet and timid like Alice's Cheshire cat
She wore stilettoes to a storm site. Who does that?

Unbothered that her soulmate has been cheating
Gained the public's empathy, but it was self-defeating
She spends her personal time taking care of her son
And appears unfazed by the damage Trump has done

We believe she hasn't a clue and prefers to ignore
That petty inscription on the cheap coat she wore
Most women are born with a loving, warm heart
Michelangelo didn't make Melania. She's no work of art

Passive-Aggressive

Hide in dark shadows, wish they had the nerve
To say what they feel their tongue on the verge
Telling others off give them a piece of their mind
An alliance with passive-aggressive is hard to find

Passive-aggressive people instigate deceptive games
They are manipulators proficient at casting blame
Pretend to be a team player but won't participate
When you learn the truth, it's too little, too late

Give others the cold shoulder makes a good actor
Claim to have your back but only for a favor
Lavish on phony praise while inflicting harm
Their most dominant feature is to remain calm

Quick to give advice but avoid commitment
Romantic or platonic signals are resentment
Will argue with a stop sign believe they can win
In my personal opinion, they are hostile friends

They are always non-compliant, refuse to try
Promise you can count on them, but again, they lie
Suppress their frustration until the big reveal
Almost snap off their arm before they say how they feel

I hope you are never victimized by one of them
They smile in your face, behind your back, condemn
Thumbs always down will not let anyone succeed
Passively cut your throat, just to watch you bleed

Souls on Board

At Dover, we greet them to say goodbye
Families come, their remains to retrieve
Fallen are escorted with honor and pride
As we mourn and comfort their bereaved

Each closely guarded, no one is allowed
To engage or handle the precious cargo
American flag drapes like a shroud
A son or a daughter we will never know

They fought gallantly, sacrificed their lives
Dignified transfers from the public's sight
They are now immortal, soaring to the skies
Their souls on board; spirits taken flight

Dedicated to those who killed in action during combat

You Are, I Am

Native-born, illegal, immigrant, and naturalized
Brown skin, blond hair, high cheekbones, almond eyes
From Times Square to the Golden Gates out West
Some cursed by hardship; others richly-blessed

From G.I., Silent, Boomers, Millennials, Gen X to Z
Land of the free, home of the slave, but no tyranny
The flag we wave is bloody red, white, and blue
Protest in the streets affirm our point of view

Christians, atheists, Muslims, Buddhists, and Jews
Classical, hip hop, country, gospel, jazz, rhythm and blues
Army, Navy, Marines, Coast Guard, Airforce our defenders
Most served with honor and pride; there were a few pretenders

Bank of America, Chase, Ally, Alliant, and Discover®
The top five financial giants have recovered
Claimed victims of recession received a big bailout
The most vulnerable among us don't have much clout

Democrats, Republicans, Independents, Socialists, and Klan
Every political party touting its brand
They are power-hungry, flexing for dominion
Want authority and to promote their own opinion

A plethora of dialects from every part of the earth
Come to this great nation to see what it is worth
Bring their bags of suffering, yearning to breathe free
Hope at the end of their rainbow isn't a pot of poverty

About the Author

Carolyn is originally from Hall's Hill, a once small all-black enclave surrounded by a white upper-middle-class community in North Arlington, Virginia.

Carolyn grew up in a closely-knit, well-established village sustained by black business owners and productive residents from all walks of life. She remembers the oppressed systemic racism during the 1950s and the volatile civil rights movement during the 1960s. In 1959, the community's undaunted civic association leaders fought Arlington County School Board to legalize the first four young black students from Hall's Hill to integrate an all-white school system. This ground-breaking effort made national news and set a precedence for school integration throughout the state. She also remembers many of her neighbors attending the March on Washington in 1963. She wanted to go, but her mama feared for her safety.

Sadly, as a child growing up in the Jim Crow era, she carries a festered memory of a cinderblock wall separating white and black communities, which still stands as a bold-face spectacle instigating a racist tradition. The wall is a salt-in-the-wound, in-your-face—as blatant an insult as the confederate monuments erected on federal lands in and around Washington, DC metropolitan area.

These early memories influenced her to share her thoughts and feelings of racism and segregation through a black prism in her poetry. She doesn't see herself physically participating in marches but instead wields her pen as a form of protest against injustice.

Carolyn's 5th-grade teacher introduced her to black poetry at John M. Langston Elementary School, where she learned about great African American poets. This discovery inspired her to memorize and recite the black dialect poetry of Paul Laurence Dunbar, which she continues to enjoy to this day.

After thirty years employed by the federal government, she retired in 1998 and worked an additional twenty years in the private sector before completing her career in September 2015.

Carolyn and her husband, Jerry, reside in Saint Louis, MO. She is still a "Virginia girl," taking up space in a Missouri world.

In 1981, Carolyn began writing poetry for her expression and enjoyment and found it healing and therapeutic, like maintaining a diary. She enjoys providing colorful descriptions of race, relationships, politics, social issues, and the harsh reality of living in a society that views African-Americans like "*grannie's worn-out quilts.*"

Why publish a book of poetry at seventy-one? Why not! Biblically speaking, seven is a spiritual number that represents the completion of divine fulfillment. That adage, "*You're never too old, and it's never too late,*" is so true. And, after compiling well over two-hundred poems, what better time to birth a body of work when it was the spirit that initially inspired her!

Carolyn's poetry can be hard-hitting and straight-forward as she unveils the deception of men's hearts through racism and irrational dysfunction. However, it also expresses compassion, hope, love, and devotion through the interaction of family, friends, and strangers.

Carolyn hopes that her poetry tapestry is worth the read.

Made in the USA
Middletown, DE
14 February 2021

33278109R10123